SALES LINKAGE: Why Do I Need an Umbrella?

Patrick M. Arcement

2026

Table of Contents

SALES LINKAGE: Why Do I Need an Umbrella?

Teach Yourself (or Anyone) How to Sell the Right Way
Using Psychology and Needs-Based Selling

Patrick M. Arcement
Edited by Melissa W. Arcement

SparkUS Publications · 2026

Copyright

SALES LINKAGE: Why Do I Need an Umbrella?

Teach Yourself (or Anyone) How to Sell the Right Way — Using Psychology and Needs-Based Selling

This book is a work of non-fiction. While every effort has been made to ensure accuracy, the author and publisher make no representations or warranties regarding the completeness or accuracy of the contents herein. The strategies and examples are illustrative and not guarantees of success. Readers are encouraged to adapt these principles to their unique situations. Patrick is confident in this process, as it has served him well, and he wishes you wild success in your career.

SparkUS Publications · 2026 | PatrickMArcement.com

Dedication

"With God all things are possible."
(Matthew 19:26)

This book is dedicated to God, who has given us all grace — without it we would have no hope.

From our Father in Heaven, all blessings and talents flow:
"Every good gift and every perfect gift is from above, coming down from the Father of lights, with whom there is no variation or shadow due to change."
(James 1:17)

"I can do all things through Christ who strengthens me."
(Philippians 4:13)

To my wife, **Melissa**, who encouraged me repeatedly to write this book. Thank you for being my greatest supporter, cheerleader, and a true gift from God. Your unwavering belief in me has been a constant source of strength and inspiration. I appreciate you and thank you.

And to my three wonderful children, Jacob, Claire, and Rachel:
You may never fully know how much you have inspired me to be better. I love you all very much. It has been an honor and a joy to be blessed with such amazing kids, and I am proud to honor you here. I look forward to witnessing many more chapters unfold in your lives.

All glory goes to God.

Acknowledgments

To the thousands of students who gave the Sales Linkage Process a chance to take off, grow, and prove itself, this book exists because of you. Every question you asked, every objection you raised, and every breakthrough you had in the classroom helped shape this work into what it is today. The wild success we experienced together is one of the main reasons I wrote this book, so others can experience success as well.

Thank you.

Preface

Why Sales Is an Honorable Trade

Sales is more than a profession; it is a life skill. It shapes how we communicate, how we listen, and how we solve problems in every area of life. Done right, selling is not about persuasion or pressure. It is about understanding, guiding, and helping people get what they truly need. You become a consultant, not a pusher.

This book draws from over two decades of experience in sales, coaching, and leadership. It offers actionable strategies, proven tools, and practical techniques that improve performance while building stronger relationships. My goal is to give you a clear, repeatable process you can use not only to close deals but to elevate every conversation you have.

Success in sales — and in life — comes from active listening, asking the right questions, and providing solutions people genuinely value. The most effective sales professionals are not pushy persuaders; they are trusted advisors who earn credibility through problem-solving, not pressure.

Every principle, story, and exercise in this book leads to one framework, a process designed to make selling feel natural, authentic, and repeatable. At the heart of this book is the **Sales Linkage Process**. It integrates psychology, relationship-building, and real-world experience into a GPS for every conversation, guiding you toward trust, value, and results. It is structured enough to give direction, yet flexible enough to adapt to any customer or situation.

I wrote this book after years of watching talented people struggle, not because they lacked skill, but because they misunderstood what sales truly is. My hope is to help you rediscover the honor, purpose, and joy that comes from serving others through sales.

Whether you are brand new to sales or a seasoned professional, the lessons in these pages will give you fresh perspective, sharper skills, and a practical toolkit for success. More importantly, they will remind you why sales, when done right, is one of the most honorable trades in the world.

The title* Why Do I Need an Umbrella?** ***began as a simple question. Once you can truly answer it, it will change how you sell, how you serve, and how you see people. I wish you wild success and hope you will share your knowledge with others so they too can be great.

About the Author

Patrick M. Arcement is a father, husband, salesman, AI technologist, college instructor, and speaker who has inspired countless professionals through his courses on sales, customer service, leadership, coaching, and team building. With years of experience in both frontline sales and corporate training, he has refined methods that simplify complex strategies into easy-to-follow, result-driven processes.

Patrick serves as an instructor at Indian River State College (IRSC), where he helps students and professionals elevate their skills in real-world communication and sales. Beyond the classroom, he has partnered with business accelerator programs to support entrepreneurs and small business owners, and he has worked with municipalities to train professionals in leadership, coaching, and customer service. His career spans diverse industries, including home cleaning products, air purifiers, promotional items, smartphones, door to door campaigns, healthcare insurance, and government agencies, proving that the **Sales Linkage Process** works in every field.

Why Patrick Wrote This Book

Throughout his career, Patrick attended countless sales training sessions, but many fell short. Some were too vague, others too rigid, and most were overwhelming. None truly explained concepts in a way that felt natural or easy to deploy in the real world. As a trainer, Patrick was tasked with building a program that was easy to teach, scalable, and trackable for effectiveness. To fill that gap, Patrick created the **Sales Linkage Process**, a practical, psychology-backed approach designed to engage students rather than overwhelm them.

By studying psychology, buyer behavior, communication skills, countless data points and decision-making drivers, Patrick developed a system that equips salespeople to listen, connect, and solve real needs. His hope is that readers will gain not only valuable skills for real-life situations but also a competitive edge in the job market.

Patrick credits many mentors throughout his life for inspiring him to share his experience and write this book. His goal is simple: to help others succeed in sales and in life by teaching them a process that builds trust, solutions, and lasting relationships.

For inquiries, coaching, leadership and sales training, or to connect with Patrick:

- Personal site: patrickmarcement.com
- Book site: umbrellasalesbook.com
- Sales training programs: saleslinkageprograms.com
- AI technology: repliantarc.com
- Strategy & consulting: arcementstrategygroup.com

Patrick is also available for 1-on-1 coaching sessions. To schedule a session, visit umbrellasalesbook.com.

As a thank-you for reading: Use code **MyLinkage50** at checkout to save $50 on the full Sales Linkage online course at umbrellasalesbook.com. Valid as long as the course is available.

How to Use This Book

This book is both a read and a reference. You can work through it front to back and I recommend doing that the first time, but it is also designed so you can return to any chapter when you need it most.

Here is how to get the most out of it:

Read it actively. The Sales Linkage Process is not theory. Every chapter is built around something you can use in your next conversation. As you read, think about your specific customers, your specific objections, and your specific industry. The principles apply everywhere.

Use the worksheets. At the end of each chapter, you will find a reference to a corresponding worksheet. These are not just busy work. They are the tools that turn reading into doing. Fill them out. Practice the scripts. The salesperson who writes things down performs differently than the one who just reads.

Take the Pro Tips seriously. Each PRO TIP in this book is a condensed lesson from the field. They are short because they are precise. Read them slowly.

Let the Let's Review sections anchor you. Each chapter ends with a Let's Review page. If you are ever going back to a chapter for a quick reference, start there. It captures the most important takeaways in one place.

Bring it to your team. If you lead a sales team, this book is a coaching tool. The Umbrella Game in Chapter 12 alone is worth a team meeting. The leadership chapters are written for managers and coaches, not just individual sellers.

Use the Appendix. The back of this book contains key scripts, tools, and reference materials from every chapter. Keep them close.

One final note: this book will not make you a great salesperson by sitting on your shelf. It works when you work it.

Ready to go deeper? The full Sales Linkage online course — 18 modules, 18 worksheets, and a certificate of completion — is available at umbrellasalesbook.com. Use code **MyLinkage50** at checkout to save $50 as a thank-you for reading.

Chapter 1: Maintaining a Positive Mindset

Resilience in the Face of "No" — and Beyond

"To the worm in horseradish, the whole world is horseradish."

This quote serves as a powerful reminder that our perspective is shaped by our environment and mindset. If all you know is struggle, limitation, or negativity, it can feel like that is all there is. But what if the worm dared to look beyond the horseradish? This saying is both a warning and a call to action. It challenges us to expand our perspectives and recognize that growth comes from stepping outside of what we have always known. Whether in sales, leadership, or personal development, the world is far bigger than the horseradish we have been living in. What "horseradish" are you living in?

"What you are looking for, you will find."

This applies to every situation, including the way you speak to yourself. You can frame any situation negatively. Consider the saying, "the early bird catches the worm." One could just as easily reframe it as "the early worm gets eaten." I know this chapter is loaded with worm references, but I promise I will wrap that up soon!

Sales is a career full of opportunities, but rejection is inevitable. Maintaining a positive mindset is essential for success. Every "no" should be seen as a steppingstone rather than a roadblock. However, it is important to recognize when a "no" becomes a genuine roadblock requiring attention. When you receive a "no," pause and assess whether a better solution can address the concern. Often, a "no" can be cost-justified if a stronger "yes" exists, one that offers the customer something they value equally or even more. For instance, if a TV costs $100 more than expected but includes a free $150 streaming service, the customer gains $50 in value overall. We will explore Cost Justification in greater depth in Chapter 8. That is why it is crucial to manage one need at a time: by focusing on one need and one solution, you avoid overwhelming the customer and can address each objection individually.

One more thing: you will never become your best self if you let doubt (your own or anyone else's), set your limits. Stay away from the "what ifs" and the habit of second-guessing yourself. No one expects expert-level performance on day one, or even day ten. Work at it daily, grow a little each time, and let progress, not perfection, define your path.

Building Resilience

Rejection in sales is rarely personal. It is often a matter of timing, circumstances, or fit. Instead of dwelling on the "no," use it as a learning opportunity. Ask yourself what you could do differently next time and how you can sharpen your approach. Every rejection is a steppingstone to growth and better strategies.

I want to be very clear: you will not sell to everyone, and you will not sell every product or service to every customer. Sales is about building relationships, and sometimes those relationships need to be nurtured over time. There will be moments when you simply are not the right solution for a customer, and that is perfectly okay. Accepting this truth allows you to focus on building genuine connections with those who truly need what you offer.

One key strategy is to follow the **Sales Linkage Process**. This approach helps you qualify leads quickly and pinpoint where objections might arise, ensuring you fully understand what the customer is truly looking for. If you approach a sale with fear or desperation, you will likely abandon the process because your focus shifts from understanding customer needs to simply chasing a "yes."

Just as sunlight is known as the best disinfectant, open and honest communication is the essential light that exposes and resolves issues. Customers crave transparency, and by embracing honesty, we build trust and foster long-lasting relationships.

Let's Be Honest

While we may not sell to every customer, the Sales Linkage Process enables you to stay focused on the needs of your prospects. By avoiding tactics that merely dump features or push for a sale at any cost, you create a more meaningful dialogue. This honest, needs-focused approach will naturally lead to more frequent and more successful sales interactions.

Many current sales programs emphasize discussing a customer's buying power and budgets as an integral part of the process. However, I do not subscribe to this approach unless the customer raises it as a need or concern. I have even heard statements like, "If they don't have the money, why waste time with them?" This is an outlook I find disheartening. Rather than dismissing potential customers based on financial constraints, we should focus on building a personal brand as a solution provider who fosters long-term relationships.

If you came to this book expecting flashy, superficial tactics, this is not the right book for you. This work is designed to save you time by teaching you how to build your lead list effectively and sell using a proven process that generates more "yes" responses.

I have also observed that many sales processes fail to address critical questions, such as when to stop collecting needs or how to incorporate psychological insights into the conversation. Yes, psychology plays a significant role in every human interaction. Research suggests that attention spans are decreasing year after year. A widely cited 2015 Microsoft study found that the average human attention span had declined from 12 seconds in 2000 to 8 seconds by 2015. Although the methodology has been debated, the finding is widely used to illustrate the trend of diminishing attention spans in the digital age. In this book, we will outline five straightforward steps that drive both sales and relationship-building simultaneously while keeping the customer engaged.

Furthermore, regardless of who we are, what we do, or how we worship, we all share the same favorite topic: ourselves. People naturally enjoy talking about themselves, and as sales professionals, we should take advantage of that by encouraging our customers to share their stories. I once delivered a talk to an audience of approximately 600 people, and one audience member remarked that my approach was narcissistic. I asked, "Can you tell me why?" The person replied, "Because you do not talk about yourself." I then asked, "If not yourself, who do you talk about?" The individual responded, "I talk about my dog, my husband, and my kids." Notice the repeated use of "my." It is not about me. It is about their personal world. The takeaway is clear: if you want people to like you, talk about them. This is not only a key sales strategy but a call to action in your personal relationships, because people fundamentally desire to be heard and understood.

Maintaining a Positive Mindset in the Face of Objections

Maintaining a positive mindset when faced with objections is fundamental to your development as a salesperson. As with any discipline, achieving mastery requires continual practice and refinement. Consider that you did not learn to drive and immediately execute elaborate stunts on your very first day. Most people must practice repeatedly, focusing on the fundamentals until they develop the balance and confidence necessary for success. The same principle applies to sales: by treating each day as an opportunity for improvement, you will gradually become more composed, proficient, and effective.

Take inspiration from the story of Colonel Sanders, the founder of Kentucky Fried Chicken. While he is a household name today, Sanders endured nearly 2,000 rejections before receiving his first "yes." He traveled across the country, broke, pitching his fried chicken franchise idea, facing rejection after rejection. How many of us would have given up after 10, 50, or 100 rejections? Yet Sanders persisted, sticking to his process and pushing through rejection until he achieved success.

To be clear, I am not saying you should go broke chasing a "yes." Sometimes success requires sticking to a process, refining your skills, and pushing through rejection. I have seen firsthand how rejection can cripple people, causing them to overthink, abandon their process, and give up before they have given themselves a real chance. That is why I made this topic Chapter One: you need to stay positive throughout the entire process.

Be inspired by Sanders. Words have power, and the way you talk to yourself matters. If you say, "I can't," then you won't. Think about it. If you spoke to your friends or family the way you sometimes speak to yourself, would you still have them in your life? Probably not. Instead, be kind to yourself. Learn from setbacks, reframe rejection as experience, and stay positive while following the Sales Linkage Process.

As Maya Angelou once said, "People will forget what you said, people will forget what you did, but people will never forget how you made them feel." Remember that in every interaction, whether in sales, business, or life. Every conversation is an opportunity to create a lasting impact.

Building Lasting Relationships and Becoming a Problem Solver

Sales is not about closing deals; it is about building lasting relationships and providing tailored solutions that truly address your customers' needs. Trust takes time, and persistence is key. Even if a sale does not happen immediately, a strong, genuine relationship can lead to future opportunities. In our process, we never think of a sale as "closed." Instead, we keep doors open and guide people toward the best solutions for their needs.

Our approach is built on the understanding that sales is about seeing things from the customer's perspective, not our own. When faced with challenges or objections, we light candles in the dark rather than curse the darkness. Every interaction is an opportunity to illuminate the path forward. By focusing on the customer's unique needs, we shift from short-term wins to long-term success.

Passion in sales is more than mere enthusiasm. It is a deep commitment to helping people, positioning yourself as a trusted solution provider, and engaging in every conversation with a genuine eagerness to solve problems. Gratitude goes far beyond saying "thank you." While words are the simplest form of gratitude, the highest form is the gift of time. In sales, time translates into expertise, guidance, and support, empowering customers to make informed decisions that improve their lives.

Balancing Persistence and Knowing When to Step Back

In sales, persistence is key, but it is equally important to recognize when a "no" is final. A "no" becomes a hard "no" when we can no longer cost-justify a solution, or when the solutions we have simply will not work for the customer. Remember, the customer is in control; we are merely guides on their journey to finding the right solution.

By following the Sales Linkage Process, we trust that the process will reveal the true needs of our customers. Conducting a thorough needs analysis gives customers the opportunity to express what they value, enabling us to craft solutions with purpose. Sometimes meeting those needs requires careful cost justification; other times, it may show us that we simply do not have the right solution at that moment. This is perfectly okay, as long as we adhere to the **Sales Linkage Process**.

The key is to view every "no" as a learning opportunity. When a "no" stems from a fundamental misalignment between the customer's needs and our solutions, it is time to step back and respect their decision. Balancing persistence with the wisdom to know when to let go ensures that we focus our energy where it truly counts.

Maintaining a positive mindset is only the beginning. Optimism gives you endurance, but structure gives you direction. In the next chapter, we will look at how to channel that mindset into a clear, repeatable process: the **Sales Linkage Process**. Think of it this way: attitude is the engine, but process is the steering wheel. Without both, even the most motivated salesperson will drift off course.

PRO TIP: *Your self-talk becomes your sales talk. Before every call or customer interaction, take five seconds and say to yourself: "My job is to serve, not sell." That single mindset shift will change how you open, how you listen, and how you close. People can feel the difference between someone who needs the sale and someone who is genuinely there to help them.*

Let's Review

- Rejection is part of the process. Learn from it and move forward. Address each need individually, offer one solution at a time, and secure a "yes" for each.
- Maintain a positive mindset in the face of objections. Resilience is key. A positive mindset helps you keep moving forward and overcome challenges.
- Focus on building relationships, not just transactions. Relationships lead to repeat business and lasting partnerships.
- Position yourself as a problem solver. When you focus on needs, you stand out in a way that fosters trust, satisfaction, and growth.
- Know when to step back. A "no" is sometimes the right answer. Respecting that builds more trust than forcing a close.
- **Remember:** Attitude is the engine, but process is the steering wheel. You need both.

Chapter 2: The Sales Linkage Process

The Bridge Between Needs and Solutions

Now that we've built the mindset to handle rejection and stay positive, it's time to add structure to that optimism. Confidence without direction is just enthusiasm waiting to fade. The **Sales Linkage Process** turns that energy into a step-by-step map you can follow in every conversation.

This framework was born from a single question that reshaped how I teach sales: *"Why do I need an umbrella?"* That simple question revealed how easily people jump into selling features instead of discovering needs. Out of that exercise came a process, a linkage that connects mindset, psychology, and real-world dialogue into something repeatable, measurable, and deeply human.

The **Sales Linkage Process** is about connecting real-world needs to tailored solutions using the products or services we sell. It is a structured, relationship-centered process that helps sales professionals uncover customer needs, build trust, and deliver meaningful solutions.

I call it the Sales Linkage Process because the focus of all sales should be to create a connection between a customer's needs, wants, concerns, and dreams. Early in my career as a trainer, I would explain the concept by holding up my left hand and saying, "This is a solution," then my right hand and saying, "This is a need." Bringing my hands together created a visual link. This connection transforms a transactional encounter into a trust-based relationship, ensuring that both you and the customer are aligned in the journey toward the right solution.

A need is required to find a solution. That is our job in a nutshell.

This approach emphasizes asking open-ended questions to discover needs *before* providing solutions. Marketing tells people what to buy. It drives awareness and gets the phone to ring. Sales, on the other hand, is about asking questions and actively listening to uncover needs. The customer wants to eat, so we serve them what they want, not what we think they want.

REMEMBER: Marketing tells; sales asks.

A needs assessment is critical and must happen before attempting to offer solutions. The word "needs," or discovering them, does not even appear in most definitions of sales. Sales Linkage, however, is about learning why people are here, what they want, and what they can afford. Then link their needs to tailored solutions. Overwhelmed customers freeze, and scared people do not buy.

Each need gives you one half of a link, while the solution provides the other half. When you make enough links, you create a genuine connection with the customer. I remember being hired by a CEO to help his team understand sales. After watching him give an impressive marketing pitch, he turned to me and said, "I feature dump. I can't stop talking about what we do and how we do it. I don't allow anyone to talk because I'm too busy talking." This was my ah-ha moment. Most salespeople, when "selling," were too busy delivering their pitch and not asking needs questions. Marketing is a one-sided pitch, while sales is a two-way conversation.

If you must do both marketing and sales because you own a small business or work for a small company, that is fine. Just learn when to take the marketing hat off and put the sales hat on. If you are telling, you are not selling.

Breaking Down the Process

The **Sales Linkage Process** is divided into five key steps that build on each other, much like a GPS guiding you to your destination. A GPS does not give all the directions at once; it provides step-by-step instructions and recalibrates if you encounter a roadblock. In the same way, this process allows you to adjust and stay on course while keeping both you and the customer engaged.

The fastest way to kill a sale is to feature-dump, throwing too much information at the customer before fully understanding their needs. The Sales Linkage Process prevents this by focusing on one step at a time, ensuring that solutions are presented only after a full needs analysis has been conducted.

Key Benefits of Following the Process

- **Focus:** Present only the relevant features after thoroughly understanding the customer's needs.
- **Clarity:** Each step builds logically on the previous one.
- **Engagement:** A structured process prevents information overload for both parties.

The 5 Steps of the Sales Linkage Process

1. **Who Am I and Why You Need Me:** Start by introducing yourself and establishing credibility. Use the customer's name throughout the process to build rapport. This includes the commitment statement explained in Chapter 3.

2. **Use Their Name:** Once you discover their name in the introduction, use it. Make it feel like a normal conversation, not a sales pitch. Using their name demonstrates that you are listening and keeps things warm and personal.

3. **Find the Need:** Use open-ended questions to uncover the customer's challenges and priorities. Let them guide the conversation.

4. **Offer a Solution:** Present a solution that directly addresses their needs, avoiding unnecessary feature-dumping.

5. **Check for Agreement:** Ask questions like, "How does that sound?" to confirm understanding and build momentum.

6. **Address Gaps with Cost Justification:** Highlight value and long-term savings to bridge any cost discrepancies.

7. **Assume the Sale:** Use action statements to move confidently into the next steps.

The Psychology Behind the Process

Understanding why this format works is just as important as knowing how to use it. When you meet a customer, they are typically in cognitive load mode, problem-solving, feeling mild anxiety, and experiencing uncertainty about whether you can help them. The Sales Linkage Process is designed to neutralize all three of those mental states, one step at a time.

Step 1 exists to lower emotional friction, so the customer is mentally available for the conversation. Until this happens, the customer is not ready to answer questions, evaluate options, or make decisions. When people contact a salesperson, their brain quietly runs one instant filter: "Is this person here to execute my decision or improve it?" If the salesperson does not establish expertise early, the customer automatically labels them as an order taker. Once that label is set, customers tend to withhold context and answer questions with the bare minimum.

That is why role definition must happen first. Who Am I, and Why Am I Important to You? comes before Find Needs. You earn the right to ask better questions and bring better options. An order taker sells exactly what the customer asks for. A salesperson prevents the customer from unintentionally under-utilizing the solution and ending up with buyer's remorse.

When you reach the needs phase, questions exist to identify all needs, avoid rework, and build confidence in the solution. Then active listening does the heavy lifting. We repeat what the customer says because paraphrasing can feel dismissive, while repetition confirms accuracy. Customers trust what sounds like their own words, and that creates perceived competence.

Once you have asked the right questions and fully understood the needs, you do not present this or that. You present the right answer. You present what fits them best. When people face too many choices, anxiety rises and they either delay or disengage. Guidance works because the solution is anchored in the customer's own words. The path feels logical instead of sales-driven, and the salesperson is positioned as an expert advisor.

"Connection calms them, needs clarify them, solutions guide them, and the final step simply secures the decision."

PRO TIP: *If you are ever unsure where you are in the process, ask yourself one question: "Have I uncovered at least three real needs?" If the answer is no, you are not ready to present solutions yet. Go back and ask more questions. Most sales are lost because someone moved to solutions too fast, not because the product was wrong.*

Let's Review

- Introduce yourself and establish credibility first, before anything else.
- Make The Commitment: clearly state your role and intentions from the outset.
- Conduct a thorough needs analysis: use active listening and open-ended questions to uncover 3–5 key needs.
- Link solutions to needs: present each solution individually and provide cost justification as needed.
- Check for agreement continuously: gather multiple "yes" responses to build momentum and confidence.
- Assume the sale confidently: transition naturally to action once the customers' needs are fully addressed.
- **Marketing tells; sales asks. If you are telling, you are not selling.**

Chapter 3: Sales Linkage Step 1 — Opening with Reason and Commitment

The initial phase of the Sales Linkage Process has gone by several names: Who Am I and Why Am I Important to You, The Reason and Commitment, and simply Opening. Each of these terms is accurate because this step is more than just an introduction. It is the foundation upon which the entire sales relationship is built. Like any meaningful interaction, it begins with a solid introduction, ensuring that the customer knows both our name and our role. More importantly, it establishes us as subject matter experts, reassuring the customer that they are in capable hands.

However, this step goes beyond personal introductions. It includes The Reason and Commitment. It is a crucial element that prevents the conversation from spiraling into confusion or uncertainty. Acknowledging the customer's reason for seeking assistance ensures they feel heard and understood. If we fail to address their initial need, we risk losing control of the interaction, forcing the customer to over-explain or take charge themselves.

The Commitment: A Foundation for Trust and Structure

At its core, *The Commitment* represents a fundamental promise that sales professionals make to both themselves and their customers. It is more than a procedural obligation; it is a pledge to engage with authenticity, integrity, and unwavering dedication throughout every phase of the sales process.

Effectively, The Commitment verbalizes the steps of the Sales Linkage Process, ensuring clarity and alignment from the outset. Consider this structured example:

Salesperson:

1. Restate the known need: *"It would be an absolute pleasure to help you find a plan that includes your doctors and medications."*

2. Introduce yourself and establish expertise: *"My name is Patrick, and I'm a licensed healthcare advocate."*

3. Set expectations: *"Today, I will ask you a few needs-based questions…"*

4. Clarify the process: *"…so we can identify the best solutions tailored to your situation."*

5. Define the path forward: *"Once you feel that the solutions meet your needs, we can move forward with securing your coverage. How does that sound?"*

Before diving into needs analysis and solutions, position yourself as an expert. This introductory step is all about establishing trust and credibility. Every relationship begins with a clear introduction, and using the customer's name throughout the conversation helps create a personal connection.

Additional Example

"It's nice to meet you, Mrs. Johnson. I'm Patrick, and today I will be your [realtor, insurance agent, custom floor builder, timepiece concierge]. My role is to help you find the right solution that meets your needs and fits your goals. I'm a certified advisor with over 10 years of experience helping families like yours make confident decisions."

This brief but impactful introduction reassures the customer that they're collaborating with a trusted expert. This is also the moment to position yourself as the expert. If you hold certifications, licenses, or unique qualifications, mention them here. The more specific your introduction, the more memorable you will be.

From "The Commitment" to "My Commitment"

Here is where ownership changes everything.

During a journey to a tradeshow, a paramedic colleague and I encountered a traffic accident. Without hesitation, he insisted on stopping, citing an oath he had taken. He parked our vehicle at a safe distance and ran back to the scene to assist. He attended to a woman with a minor facial burn from an airbag deployment. Upon the arrival of on-duty paramedics, he briefed them and returned to our car.

Curious about the "oath" he mentioned, I asked further. He explained that, as a paramedic, he is bound by a commitment to provide care in emergencies, regardless of the circumstances.

The Emergency Medical Technician Oath includes the promise: *"Be it pledged as an Emergency Medical Technician; I will honor the physical and judicial laws of God and man. I will follow that regimen which, according to my ability and judgment, I consider for the benefit of patients…"*

Reflecting on this, I realized that sales professionals should adopt a similar commitment to assist those in need. Just as paramedics are driven by their oath to provide immediate care, sales professionals are called to respond to the needs of their clients with dedication and integrity.

Will you answer the call?

The key transition is moving from referring to this as *The Commitment* to embracing it as **My Commitment**. By stating the commitment aloud, we reinforce our role and establish a positive framework for the conversation. This verbalization strengthens our professional confidence, ensures consistency, and systematically aligns each interaction with the Sales Linkage Process. More importantly, it builds trust with the customer, positioning us as advisors rather than mere salespeople.

Once we have taken control and set a clear path, we can focus on identifying the customer's needs. By proactively guiding the discussion, we create an environment in which the customer feels supported, reducing uncertainty and hesitation. This structured approach naturally leads to the next phase: uncovering all relevant needs, making meaningful connections between solutions and concerns, and ultimately delivering a personalized, value-driven experience.

Incorporating My Commitment into every conversation is not just a best practice. It is a transformative approach that fosters trust, clarifies expectations, and drives successful outcomes. By embracing this framework, sales professionals ensure consistency, enhance customer confidence, and effectively link customer needs to the most suitable solutions.

The Customer Sentiment Health Bar

Imagine customer sentiment as the health bar of a video game character. Every interaction either fills up or drains that bar. Each action, whether big or small, contributes points toward building trust and loyalty, or subtracts points and chips away at your overall relationship.

Just as a video game character might receive a bonus health boost at the start of a level, a strong initial customer experience can give you an early advantage. Research supports the power of first impressions: a PwC study found that 73% of consumers consider the initial customer experience a critical factor in shaping their overall perception of a brand and salesperson.

Every touchpoint, from a friendly greeting on your website to the tone of an email follow-up, acts like a small hit or bonus in the game. According to Deloitte, nearly 80% of customers evaluate every single interaction with a brand as an indicator of its overall quality. This means that even seemingly minor missteps can subtract points from your sentiment health bar, while consistently positive engagements build a robust, healthy relationship.

American Express reports that a dissatisfied customer is likely to share their negative experience with 15 or more people, illustrating how one "critical hit" can ripple through your customer base. The goal is to keep that bar as full as possible, ensuring your customers not only stay engaged but also become loyal advocates for your brand.

Overcoming Fear and Establishing Control

Salespeople often lose control of the conversation if fear takes over. Our "cave brain" is wired for self-preservation; when we face uncertainty, our minds tend to jump to worst-case scenarios. We instinctively seek to avoid harm, surprises, or any potential threats, much like the unsettling feeling you get in a dark room before the light comes on.

To illustrate this concept, imagine a dark room. Darkness can be unsettling, especially if you hear a sudden thud in the middle of the night. Until you identify the source of the noise, your mind might race through countless worst-case scenarios. This natural tendency to fill in the blanks with negative assumptions highlights a critical truth: in the absence of a story, people create their own. And it is usually a bad one.

The same principle applies to your customers. Every customer carries an invisible "backpack" filled with negative experiences from past customer service or sales encounters. The moment a salesperson does anything that remotely resembles those negative interactions, the customer assumes they are in for another unpleasant experience. This is precisely why The Commitment, now **My Commitment**, is so essential. It turns the light on in that dark room before the customer's imagination does it for them.

Never Say "That"

Words matter in sales. A common mistake is saying, "I can help you with that," which adds little value. Instead, use the Statement-Question Linking technique to restate the customer's words before smoothly transitioning to the next question. This demonstrates active listening and keeps the dialogue dynamic. We discuss this further in Chapter 9.

PRO TIP: *Practice your Commitment out loud before every shift or sales session. It should sound natural, not scripted. Record yourself once and listen back. If it sounds like a robot reading a policy, rewrite it in your own voice. The Commitment works because it sounds like a real person who genuinely wants to help. Authenticity cannot be faked, but it can be practiced.*

Let's Review

- The Opening establishes credibility and sets the tone for everything that follows.
- The Commitment is a structured promise to the customer. It eliminates fear, sets expectations, and establishes your role as an advisor, not a pusher.
- **The Commitment becomes My Commitment.** Own it, internalize it, and say it like you mean it every single time.
- Using the customer's name frequently personalizes the interaction and signals that you are truly listening.
- The Customer Sentiment Health Bar reminds us that every touchpoint adds or subtracts from the relationship. Start strong.
- Without My Commitment, the customer's imagination fills the silence, usually with something negative. Turn the light on.

Chapter 4: Sales Linkage Step 2 — Identifying Needs: The Diagnostic Phase

Once introductions are complete and My Commitment has been established, the next step is to discover the customer's needs. Without a clear diagnostic phase, it is impossible to provide tailored solutions or demonstrate value. In this phase, you are not selling. You are actively listening.

Think of yourself as a doctor conducting a patient consultation. A good doctor does not walk into the room and immediately start prescribing medication. They ask questions. They listen. They dig deeper to understand what is truly going on before making any recommendations. That is exactly what we do in the needs phase. We diagnose before we prescribe.

"Can you tell me more about what's driving your search for a solution?"

Why 3–5 Needs?

Psychological research supports limiting the number of key items a person can process. According to Miller's Rule of 7 (often referred to as "chunking"), people can hold only about five to nine items in their working memory at one time. In practice, I have found that focusing on three to five key needs strikes the perfect balance, uncovering meaningful insights while keeping the conversation manageable and preventing the customer from becoming overwhelmed.

Many students have asked, "When a patient is taking five or six medications, does that mean they have five or six needs?" The answer is no. It represents one need: the need for medication. Although this single need manifests in multiple components, we address each part one at a time in our solutions.

Summary: Limiting needs to 3–5 ensures you capture meaningful insights while keeping the customer engaged.

Asking Effective Open-Ended Questions

Open-ended questions are your most powerful tool for uncovering needs. Unlike yes/no questions, they encourage the customer to elaborate, providing valuable insights:

1. *"What's most important to you when choosing [product/service]?"*
2. *"Can you tell me about the challenges you're facing right now?"*
3. *"What's worked well for you in the past, and what hasn't?"*
4. *"How do you see this solution fitting into your goals?"*
5. *"What's your biggest priority at the moment?"*
6. *"Are there specific features or benefits you're looking for?"*
7. *"How does your current situation compare to what you'd like it to be?"*
8. *"What is your biggest challenge right now?"*
9. *"Can you describe the ideal outcome for you?"*
10. *"What's motivated you to explore [product/service] now?"*

These questions not only reveal practical needs but also help tap into the emotional drivers behind a customer's decision-making process. Research indicates that nearly 90% of consumers trust companies whose service they rate as "very good" to take care of their needs. Moreover, 88% of customers are more likely to make repeat purchases from companies that offer excellent customer service. Both of those outcomes start here, in the needs phase.

Overcoming Objections During the Needs Phase

Inevitably, some customers will raise objections even during the needs discovery phase. Instead of viewing these as barriers, reframe them as opportunities to clarify how your solution meets their needs. For example: *"I understand your concern about the upfront cost. Many of my clients have discovered that, when considering the long-term savings and the peace of mind this solution provides, it actually proves more economical over time. Would you like me to demonstrate how these savings accumulate?"*

A common objection I frequently encounter is, *"I need to talk to my spouse about this."* I prefer to ask questions to gain further insight: *"What objections do you think they might have?"* If the customer is unsure, I suggest offering to speak with the spouse directly. If this is the right solution, my job is to help them get it.

Addressing Gaps with Cost Justification

Sometimes a customer's needs and the solution you offer may not align perfectly. This is where cost justification comes in, reframing the value so that the customer sees the benefits despite a slightly higher cost. For instance: *"I understand this plan is $20 more than you anticipated, but it includes [specific feature] that you are already paying for separately. Over time, this will actually save you $200 a year."*

By addressing each need individually, you can pause when an objection arises, address it immediately, and reinforce the overall value of the solution.

PRO TIP: *After you ask an open-ended question, count silently to five before speaking again. Most salespeople fill silence too quickly and accidentally answer their own question, robbing the customer of the opportunity to share something important. Silence is not awkward; it is productive. The customer is thinking. Let them.*

Let's Review

- The Diagnostic Phase is about asking, not telling. You are a doctor before you are a prescriber.
- Gather 3–5 key needs, not more. Depth over breadth keeps the customer focused and prevents them from being overwhelmed.
- Open-ended questions are your most powerful tool. They invite elaboration and reveal the real story.
- Objections during the needs phase are not stop signs. They are directional signals. Follow them.
- Cost justification is most effective when applied to a specific, already-identified need. Never use it as a general defense of price.
- **Remember:** You cannot link a solution to a need you have not discovered yet.

Chapter 5: Sales Linkage Step 3 — Making the Link Between Need and Solution: The Prescription Phase

Sales Is Solutions and Service

The word "sales" is thought to originate from the Old Norse word *selja*, meaning "to give" or "to serve." Whether or not that etymology holds, it underscores an essential truth: sales is about serving others. You are not there to push your agenda; you are there to advocate for the customer's needs and provide solutions that genuinely benefit them. By adopting a servant mindset, you position yourself as a trusted advisor. This advisor listens actively, empathizes with challenges, and focuses on the customer's goals rather than your own.

The Prescription Phase

Now it is time to bridge the gap between the needs you have uncovered and the solutions you offer. This is where *Sales Linkage* happens. It connects real customer needs with the most appropriate solutions. Your job is to present a solution that directly addresses each identified need, handling one solution at a time.

Think back to the doctor analogy from Chapter 4. The doctor listened, asked questions, and diagnosed the problem. Now they are writing the prescription. But notice: they do not prescribe five things at once. They address the most pressing issue first, confirm that it makes sense, and then move on to the next concern. That is exactly how we present solutions in the Sales Linkage Process.

Presenting Solutions Individually

Delivering solutions one at a time allows you to gain agreement on each point before moving forward, preventing confusion and ensuring the customer remains engaged. This methodical approach avoids choice overload, a phenomenon in which presenting too many options at once leads to decision paralysis.

Instead of overwhelming customers with a barrage of features, tailor your explanation to demonstrate precisely how each solution resolves their specific concern. For example:

"Based on what you've told me, this solution ensures you'll save money while getting the service you need. It fits within your budget. How does that sound?"

By addressing each need individually, you create a structured and positive decision-making environment, allowing the customer to confirm their agreement with each step. Each confirmation is a link in the chain. The more links you build, the stronger the connection. The more links you build, the more natural the close becomes.

Avoiding Feature-Dumping and Using Cost Justification

A common mistake salespeople make is feature-dumping. Feature-dumping means listing every benefit of a product without connecting it to the customer's specific needs. To avoid this, focus on how the solution directly addresses their concerns. If cost appears to be an issue, cost justification becomes essential:

"I understand that price is a consideration. But when you look at the added value, such as [X, Y, Z], this solution actually saves you money in the long run."

However, cost justification can only be effective if you have conducted a thorough needs assessment. Knowing all the customer's needs beforehand allows you to demonstrate value, rather than attempting to justify the cost after the fact.

Using Checking Questions to Validate Solutions

To ensure that each proposed solution is aligned with the customer's expectations, incorporate checking questions. These questions engage the customer in the process, reinforcing their role in the decision-making journey while providing immediate feedback:

- *"Does this option address the challenges we discussed?"*
- *"How do you feel this solution fits your requirements?"*
- *"Based on what you shared with me, does this make sense for your situation?"*

These questions confirm whether you've successfully met the customer's needs. If they respond with a "yes," you've successfully delivered a solution. If not, their response presents an objection, not as a rejection, but as an opportunity to refine your approach.

Turning Objections into Opportunities

Objections should never be seen as roadblocks but rather as signals that the customer still requires further clarification or reassurance. When handled correctly, objections provide insight into additional needs that may not have been fully addressed. Research shows that 88% of customers are more likely to make repeat purchases from companies that excel in providing personalized solutions. By presenting solutions individually, validating them with checking questions, and handling objections effectively, you maintain control and create a customer-centric experience that drives engagement and builds trust.

PRO TIP: When you present a solution, say the customer's name first. "Mrs. Johnson, based on what you shared about needing something reliable and easy to maintain, I believe this option is the right fit for you." Using their name anchors the solution to them personally, not to a product catalog. That single habit increases agreement rates and makes every recommendation feel genuine, not generic.

Let's Review

- Present solutions one at a time, just as a doctor prescribes one medication at a time. It prevents a customer from being overwhelmed and builds agreement step by step.
- Avoid feature-dumping. Every feature you mention should connect directly to a need the customer already expressed.
- Use checking questions after every solution. They are not interrogation. They are confirmation.
- Cost justification is most powerful after the need has already been identified and the solution has been presented.
- Objections during this phase are opportunities, not obstacles. They reveal what still needs to be addressed.
- **Remember:** The goal is not to impress the customer with what you know. It is to make them feel confident in what they are deciding.

Chapter 6: Sales Linkage Step 4 — Securing Agreement and Moving to Action

The Bridge Between Agreement and Action

The goal of every great sales conversation is not persuasion. It is alignment. When you've done your job through the earlier steps of the Sales Linkage Process — discovering needs, linking solutions, and handling objections — the close should never feel forced. It should feel like the next natural step.

In this final stage of the process, you confirm alignment through checking questions and then guide the customer into action by assuming the sale. Together, these create a smooth, confident close built on trust rather than pressure. This is also the moment where staying on offense and leading with solutions, not limitations, becomes the difference between a "yes" and a "let me think about it."

1. Why Checking Questions Matter

Checking questions are short, strategic prompts that confirm you've accurately understood and met the customer's needs. They accomplish three things:

- **Validate understanding:** you confirm that your solution matches what they asked for.
- **Engage the customer:** you invite participation rather than lecturing.
- **Reveal remaining concerns:** if hesitation appears, you can address it before it becomes an objection.

Think of checking questions as checkpoints on your GPS route. Each "yes" is a turn in the right direction, confirming you're still on course.

Examples:

- *"Does this solution meet your expectations?"*
- *"How does that sound to you?"*
- *"Would this address what we discussed earlier about [need]?"*

If the customer answers "yes," move forward. If they hesitate, switch to an open-ended follow-up:

- *"What about this doesn't feel right to you?"*
- *"Can you tell me more about what you were expecting?"*

2. Moving Naturally into Action

When each solution has been confirmed, it is time to take the next step. Because the customer has already agreed that your solution meets their needs, moving forward is simply the logical conclusion. You are not forcing a decision; you are facilitating one.

Imagine a waiter who has just taken your order. They do not ask, "Are you sure you want that?" They write it down and place it confidently. That is what this step feels like in sales: calm, natural progress built on prior agreement.

Examples in action:

- *"You've confirmed this meets all your needs. Let's secure it today so you can start seeing results."*

- *"Since this plan covers everything, we discussed, I'll go ahead and finalize it for you."*
- *"You mentioned wanting this in place by next week. Let's schedule your setup for Tuesday or Thursday. What works better?"*

3. Staying on Offense: Leading with Solutions, Not Limitations

Staying on offense means maintaining control of the conversation and keeping the focus on solutions. Many salespeople unintentionally fall into a defensive mindset when faced with objections or challenges, which can lead to hesitation, feature-dumping, or worse, losing the customer's trust.

To stay on offense, focus on what you can do for the customer rather than dwelling on what you cannot.

Instead of: "Unfortunately, that feature isn't available."
Say: "Here's how we can achieve your goal using the options we have."

This subtle shift in language keeps the conversation productive and solution oriented. Words like "solution," "benefit," and "value" shift the focus away from products and features and toward the bigger picture. Avoid words like "maybe" or "but," which can create doubt or sound confrontational.

When I was a trainer, I kept a small picture of a head of lettuce next to the clock in my classroom as a playful reminder to say "Let us" rather than issue commands because "Let us" creates a sense of teamwork and inclusion, reminding everyone that we are on the same side working toward a common goal.

4. Power Words and Action Statements

Once you have confirmed agreement, guide the customer confidently forward:

- *"This is exactly what you're looking for. Let's get the paperwork started."*
- *"Everything lines up perfectly with what you need. Let's go ahead and lock this in."*
- *"You're going to love this. I'll get things moving for you now."*
- *"Since this checks all your boxes, I'll finalize it for you."*
- *"Great choice! Let's make it official."*
- *"This solution fits everything we talked about, so let's move forward."*

The key takeaway: Confidence is contagious. When you've done a thorough needs analysis and provided a tailored solution, there's no reason to second-guess. A hesitant close plants doubt, while a firm and natural transition makes the next step feel obvious.

Think of it this way: you offered candy to someone and they already said yes. Why would you then ask, "Are you sure?" Stop re-opening closed doors.

5. Why This Works

- **Reduces Decision Fatigue:** You've already simplified choices by addressing one need at a time. Now the sale feels easy.
- **Builds Confidence:** You project professionalism and clarity, reassuring the customer they're making a sound decision.

- **Maintains Momentum:** Checking questions keep the energy alive so the close doesn't stall.
- **Eliminates Pressure:** The sale feels like the customer's idea because it is.

Research shows that more than half of customer loyalty is influenced by the sales experience itself, not just the product. When you close confidently and respectfully, you strengthen that experience.

6. Common Pitfalls to Avoid

- **Skipping Confirmation:** Don't rush to close before securing agreement. Every skipped "yes" becomes a potential "no" later.
- **Re-selling After Agreement:** Once the customer says yes, stop talking. Adding new information can create doubt.
- **Over-apologizing:** Confidence is contagious. If you sound unsure, the customer will be too.
- **Defending Instead of Leading:** When faced with a concern, lead with a solution, not a justification.
- **Leading with Negatives:** Never start a response with what you cannot do. Always lead with what you can.

PRO TIP: *You don't need permission to do your job. You earned it by getting their needs out and finding solutions for them. The "YES" answers you got to each solution? That was the "YES" you were looking for. The close is not a separate event. It is simply the last confirmation in a series of confirmations. If you have been collecting "yes" throughout the process, the close is already done. Now - read that again. Slowly. It's big.*

Let's Review

- Use checking questions after every solution to validate understanding.
- Treat each "yes" as progress toward the final close.
- When all needs are met, guide the customer naturally into action using confident action statements.
- Stay on offense. Lead with what you can do, not what you cannot.
- Replace defensive language with solution language at every turn.
- Confidence replaces pressure when you've earned agreement step by step.
- The sale should feel like the customer's decision because it is.
- **PRO TIP reminder:** You don't need permission to do your job. You earned it.

Chapter 7: Mastering the Hook, Navigating Gatekeepers, and Getting to the Sale

Creating Curiosity, Building Connection, and Opening the Door

Sales is all about creating meaningful connections that open the door to understanding and ultimately solving your prospect's problems. In this chapter, we explore how to use a well-crafted hook in various sales environments, whether you're knocking on doors, making a cold call, dealing with gatekeepers, or engaging with prospects at trade shows and events. The hook is a critical tool to start the Sales Linkage Process. Without the hook, you may be shut out before the conversation even begins.

It is important to note that a hook will often sound like marketing, because like marketing, it is designed to motivate people to act and initiate the discussion that leads to the full Sales Linkage Process. The difference is that the hook is a bridge, not a pitch. It creates permission, not pressure.

What Is a Hook?

A hook is a concise, compelling opening statement designed to capture your prospect's attention and invite them into a conversation. It is not about launching directly into a sales pitch. Instead, a well-crafted hook sets the stage for trust and curiosity. It acknowledges the prospect's current situation and frames the dialogue around their needs. The hook should always include a caring, beneficial question that helps or provides useful information. This is not the time to be pushy. We are simply here to help and educate the customer. In short, the hook is your way of saying, *"I'm here to help. Let's talk."*

The Psychology Behind Attention

People decide in seconds whether to stay engaged. In those first moments, their brains are asking three questions simultaneously: Is this person safe? Is this relevant to me? Do I want to keep listening? That means tone, clarity, and confidence matter more than any script. You are not trying to impress. You are trying to connect.

When your voice carries warmth, professionalism, and purpose, you earn permission to move forward. When it sounds scripted, rushed, or sales-driven, the door closes before you ever had a chance to walk through it.

The Elements of a Strong Hook

1. **Who you are:** *"Hi, this is [Name] with [Company Name]…"*
2. **Why you're reaching out:** *"…I'm reaching out because I noticed your company recently ordered tumblers for an event…"*
3. **What's in it for them:** *"…and I wanted to share a quick idea that could help your next order stand out and save a little on cost."*

That is it. Under 20 seconds. Clear, relevant, and inviting.

Door-to-Door Sales: Opening Doors with a Hook

Door-to-door sales come with unique challenges. Prospects are often wary of uninvited visits. Your goal is to solve problems and meet needs. Here is an example of how to engage:

"Hello, I don't know if you have noticed a lot of [BIG CABLE COMPANY] trucks in the area. We wanted to let you know that [BLANK SERVICE] is now available here, offering higher download speeds. Have you noticed any issues with your current service?"

This hook works because it informs the prospect about a new service, invites them to share their experience, and smoothly leads to a deeper, needs-based conversation. Even if the resident responds briefly or says, "I don't have time," this friendly introduction opens the door to further dialogue.

Do not be discouraged by initial setbacks. Research shows that door-to-door sales campaigns typically yield conversion rates between 1% and 3%. Knowing this upfront prevents discouragement and helps you stay focused on the process, not the outcome of any single door.

Cold Calling: Starting with a Hook

Cold calling is the practice of contacting potential customers who have not previously expressed interest in the product or service being offered. Despite its challenges, including low response rates and the prevalence of call screening, cold calling remains a critical part of many organizations' sales strategies.

Consider this example when calling a lead with past interest:

"Hello, my name is Patrick, and I'm with [BLANK]. My understanding is that you had reached out for assistance with [BLANK] at one time. Perhaps we were unable to serve you back then. May I ask if you were able to resolve that issue you were calling about?"

This approach acknowledges their past interest, builds rapport, and invites dialogue. The hook here is not meant to force a sale. It is simply the starting point for a conversation that uncovers the prospect's needs.

In the digital age, cold calling has become increasingly challenging because people now have a variety of tools to screen incoming calls. Industry research indicates that cold call answer rates can be as low as 2–5%, which underscores the rarity and importance of each successful connection. Setting realistic expectations is crucial for sustaining motivation in this demanding environment.

Gatekeepers: Navigating the First Line of Defense

In many sales environments, a gatekeeper is the person who controls access to the decision-maker. This could be a receptionist, an administrative assistant, or any front-line staff member who screens calls and manages access. Their role is to protect the decision-maker's time, not to personally stop you. Understanding this distinction changes everything.

Strategies for Getting Past Gatekeepers:

1. **Show Respect and Courtesy.** Recognize the gatekeeper's role and treat them with genuine respect. A polite greeting and a respectful tone can make a significant difference.

2. **Build Rapport.** Engage in a brief, friendly conversation: *"Good morning. I appreciate you taking my call. I know how busy things can be here."*

3. **Be Transparent but Tactful.** Clearly state your purpose without oversharing details that might trigger skepticism.

4. **Use a Compelling Hook.** *"I'm calling because we recently helped another company in your industry overcome a similar challenge. Could you advise on the best way to share some of that valuable information with the right person?"*

5. **Ask for Guidance.** *"Could you please advise me on the best time or method to speak with the person who oversees this area?"* This shows that you value their expertise and are willing to work within their system.

6. **Leverage Credibility and Social Proof.** If applicable, mention relevant credentials or success stories from similar companies. This builds trust and proves that your call has substance.

Consider the gatekeeper as a de facto decision-maker. The gatekeeper wants to be praised for bringing great ideas forward. Help them. When you make the gatekeeper look good for connecting you with the right person, you have won an ally, not just cleared an obstacle.

Trade Shows and Events: Turning Booths into Conversation Starters

Trade shows and vendor events offer a unique opportunity to engage prospects face-to-face. Often, you see amazing booths with top-notch marketing and subject matter experts standing by, but when employees do not actively interact with visitors, those opportunities walk right past.

I recommend that every company participating in trade shows or events use a hook question as people walk by. One of the best hooks I have witnessed was during an event for a company that sold air purification units for home and business use. At our booth, we held a bottle of dirty water and asked every passerby, *"Would you drink this?"* The answer was invariably a resounding "no." Then we followed up with, *"Well, did you know you're breathing it?"* This simple question immediately stopped people in their tracks. We then explained, *"This is the water we used to clean the air unit. That water came out of your air."* This powerful hook not only grabbed attention but also opened the door to a genuine conversation about air quality and the need for better purification solutions.

Hooks That Work Across Channels

Phone (Outbound or Warm Follow-Up)

"Hi [Name], this is [Your Name] with [Company Name]. I wanted to thank you again for your recent order and share a quick idea I think could complement what you already purchased."

Email or Chat

"Hello [Name], I noticed you were looking at custom water bottles for your event. Great choice. I've got a design idea that might save space and add impact. Want me to show you?"

Walk-In or Event Interaction

"I see you checking out the campfire mugs. Those are one of my favorites. What caught your eye about that style?"

Avoiding Common Hook Mistakes

- **Sounding scripted:** Readiness is good; memorization is not.
- **Starting with features:** People don't buy what something is; they buy what it does for them.
- **Talking too long:** You're seeking conversation, not compliance.

- **Ignoring tone:** Smile when you speak, as it translates through any channel.
- **Pitching too soon:** A hook earns you the right to begin Step 1. It is not Step 1 itself.

PRO TIP: *When you call someone and they say "I'm busy right now," do not apologize and hang up. Instead say, "I completely understand — I'll be brief. Would thirty seconds work?"* Nine *times out of ten they will say yes. You have just converted a rejection into a hook. From there, deliver your single most compelling sentence and ask one question. A short conversation now beats a callback that never happens.*

Let's Review

- The hook is your invitation. It earns you the right to begin the Sales Linkage Process.
- A great hook is under 20 seconds, relevant to the prospect, and ends with a question.
- Gatekeepers are allies, not obstacles. Treat them with genuine respect and help them look good.
- Door-to-door and cold calling require realistic expectations. Low response rates are normal. Stay on process.
- Trade show hooks should be interactive and challenge the prospect's current thinking.
- Tone, warmth, and brevity matter more than any script.
- **Remember:** The hook does not close the deal. It opens the door. What matters is what you do once you are inside.

Chapter 8: Cost Justification Strategies

Balancing Needs and Value — Helping Customers See Value, Not Price

Understanding the Real Objection

When a customer says, *"That's too expensive,"* it usually is not about price. It is about perception. People object when they cannot clearly see the connection between what something costs and what it is worth to them. Your job is not to defend the price. Your job is to make the value undeniable.

If the earlier steps of the Sales Linkage Process were done well, where you discovered needs and linked them to real solutions, cost justification becomes a natural conversation, not a defense. This chapter focuses on helping customers see value through their own lens, and on equipping you to handle the most common real-world price objections with confidence and care.

The Weighted Scale

Imagine every customer's decision on a scale. On one side is price; on the other is value. If the scale tips toward value, they move forward with confidence. If it tips toward price, they hesitate. Your role is not to argue about cost. It is to help them add more weight to the value side. That weight comes from relevance: how well your solution meets their specific needs, timing, or goals.

"When value is clear, price becomes secondary."

The Psychology of Value

Humans make decisions emotionally first and justify them logically second. That means your job is to help them feel confident in their choice. Then support that feeling with tangible proof. Customers want to believe they are making a smart decision. The best way to guide them there is through simple, logical comparisons that make the value obvious:

- **Contrast Effect:** Show how your solution outperforms a lower-priced alternative.
- **Future Value Framing:** Illustrate long-term savings, time saved, or risk reduced.
- **Ownership Language:** Use "when you have this" instead of "if you buy this." It shifts mindset from risk to reward.

Real Objections — and How to Handle Them

Here are the most common cost-related objections you will encounter and the Sales Linkage approach to each:

"I can get this cheaper somewhere else."
Do not argue. Acknowledge it and pivot to value: *"You absolutely can, and I want to make sure you're comparing the same thing. The option you're referencing doesn't include [specific feature the customer said was important]. Over time, the replacement cost and frustration actually make it more expensive. Can I show you the math on that?"*

"That's more than I was planning to spend."
"That's completely fair — let's talk about that. You mentioned that [specific need] is really important to you. This option is designed specifically to solve that, and here's

where it saves you money over the next 12 months... [walk through the numbers]. Does that change how you look at the cost?"

"I need to think about it."

This is rarely about thinking. It is usually about uncertainty. *"Of course — I want you to feel completely comfortable. Can I ask, is there a specific part you're still unsure about? I'd rather address that now than have you leave with a question unanswered."*

"It's not in the budget right now."

"I understand — budgets are tight for a lot of teams right now. Let me ask: when would be a better time? And in the meantime, would it help if I showed you a scaled-down option that delivers the core of what you need without the full investment?" Always keep the door open.

"I need to talk to my spouse / partner / boss."

"That makes total sense — big decisions are better made together. Can I ask, what do you think their biggest concern might be? If we can address that now, you'll be walking into that conversation with all the answers."

Making Cost Make Sense

1. **Restate the Need:** *"You mentioned needing something durable enough for daily use and easy to clean after events."*

2. **Link the Solution to the Outcome:** *"This particular option lasts twice as long as cheaper models, which means you'll replace it half as often."*

3. **Show the Math:** *"Over the next year, that's about $2 in savings per unit — and you'll avoid the frustration of having items fail mid-event."*

That is cost justification done right, not defending price but explaining value per dollar.

Words and Phrases That Build Confidence

Instead of: *"It's the best price I can do."*

Try: *"It's designed to give you the best return for what you need long-term."*

Instead of: *"That's our standard cost."*

Try: *"This includes the durability, finish, and quality you said were most important."*

Instead of: *"It might seem high at first."*

Try: *"Let me show you how this actually saves you money over time."*

Cost Justification as a Relationship Builder

When customers feel understood, they stop measuring only by price. You become someone who helps them make better decisions, not just purchases. Cost justification is not about proving value. It is about revealing it. The goal is to help them realize, *"This isn't expensive — it's worth it."*

PRO TIP: *Never apologize for your price. The moment you apologize, you signal to the customer that the price is a problem — and they will treat it like one. Instead, say it with confidence: "This option is $249 a month, and here is why that investment makes sense for you…" Confidence in your pricing signals confidence in your value. If you do not believe it is worth it, they will not either.*

Let's Review

- Value beats price when it's clear, relevant, and connected to the customer's stated needs.
- The Weighted Scale: your job is to add weight to the value side, not argue about the price side.
- Every price objection is really a value question in disguise. Answer the value question.
- *"I can get it cheaper elsewhere"* — acknowledge it, then compare the real cost including replacements, frustrations, and missed features.
- *"I need to think about it"* — find the specific uncertainty and address it directly.
- *"Not in the budget"* - offer a scaled option and keep the door open.
- Never apologize for your price. Confidence in pricing signals confidence in value.
- **Remember:** Cost justification is most powerful after the need has been identified and the solution has been presented. Sequence matters.

Chapter 9: Active Listening (Statement-Question Linked)

The Key to Understanding Needs — Listening to Understand, Not Just Respond

If the Sales Linkage Process were a house, active listening would be the foundation. Everything else we have built, the hook, the commitment, the needs phase, the solutions, the close depends entirely on your ability to hear what the customer is actually saying, not just what you expect them to say.

Think of active listening like turning the light on in that dark room we discussed in Chapter 3. When the room is dark, everyone fills the silence with their own assumptions and usually the wrong ones. However, when you truly listen, you turn the light on. The customer will tell you everything you need to know if you give them the space and the signal that you are genuinely paying attention. Great listeners do not find selling hard. They find it natural because the customer has already told them exactly what they need.

Listening Is Not Waiting to Talk

Most people believe they are good listeners, but in sales, and in life listening means more than being quiet while someone speaks. It means seeking to understand before responding. The most successful professionals do not listen to reply; they listen to connect. They do not interrupt with assumptions or rush to solve problems before hearing the full story. They listen with curiosity and precision and that is what turns conversations into relationships.

Active listening is how you uncover what truly matters to the person in front of you. It is also how you demonstrate respect without saying a single word about respect. When someone feels genuinely heard, they relax. Their defenses come down. They begin to trust you. And once trust exists, the Sales Linkage Process flows naturally.

The Psychology of Listening

The human brain processes information far faster than people speak. That gap creates temptation; we start preparing our response while the other person is still talking. The problem is, when we do that, we stop hearing what is being said.

Active listening slows that impulse. It is an intentional pause that says, *"Your words matter more than my reply."* When customers feel heard, they begin to trust. When they feel understood, they begin to act.

In neuroscience, this effect is called mirror listening. When someone repeats or reflects our thoughts back accurately, it activates our anterior insula — the empathy center of the brain. That is why listening feels good. It signals safety, care, and respect. Research shows that feeling "understood" triggers the same reward centers in the brain as receiving praise or gifts. That means every moment of genuine listening builds emotional equity, something far more valuable than a quick transaction.

The Statement-Question Linked Method

One of the most powerful tools in the Sales Linkage Process is what I call "**Statement-Question Linked."** Active listening requires proving you understand. The best way to demonstrate this is by paraphrasing what the customer has said and then linking it directly to your next question.

Example:

Customer: *"We're frustrated with our current supplier's slow turnaround."*

Salesperson: *"So speed of delivery is critical for you. How much time would you ideally like to save?"*

This technique does two things simultaneously: it validates the customer's feelings, they know you heard them, and it naturally advances the conversation toward deeper needs. By practicing **Statement-Question Linked**, you transform passive listening into active engagement, guiding the conversation with precision while building rapport.

It is not about checking boxes. It is about connecting needs to solutions in real time. I should mention this works in any relationship.

Why Statement-Question Linked Works

This method prevents the conversation from feeling like an interrogation. When you simply ask one question after another without acknowledging the customer's responses, the interaction can feel cold or transactional. The Statement-Question Linked method turns the conversation into a dialogue, creating a sense of collaboration and mutual understanding.

Additionally, repeating what the customer says forces you to truly listen. You cannot repeat or paraphrase something if you were not paying attention.

People rarely express everything they need in the first few sentences. Their initial comments are often surface-level symptoms, not the real cause. Active listening helps you uncover the deeper motivation or concern. The Statement-Question Link works because it:

- **Validates their thoughts:** *"I heard you."*

- **Invites collaboration:** *"Let's explore together."*
- **Reveals emotion behind logic:** *"Why is this important to you?"*

That is where the real sales connection happens — not in features or pricing, but in understanding the story behind the request.

Real Example: Listening Changes Everything

A customer once told me, *"We just need something quick and cheap."* Many salespeople would have gone straight to the lowest-cost product.

Instead, I replied: *"Quick and affordable, I can help. Can you tell me more about what's making speed so important right now?"*

That question opened the truth: they had an event the next week, and a past vendor had missed a delivery. What they truly valued was not cheap. It was reliability. By listening, I discovered that the pain point was not price at all. It was trust.

I could not have uncovered that by pitching features. I uncovered it by listening.

Common Mistakes That Block Connection

- **Listening to Respond, Not to Understand:** Focusing on what to say next instead of being fully present and absorbing what the other person is saying.
- **Jumping to Solutions Too Fast:** The brain loves to fix things, resist that urge until you hear the full picture.
- **Interrupting to Show Expertise:** Knowledge matters, but timing matters more.

- **Finishing Their Sentences:** It feels efficient, but it steals their ownership of the conversation.
- **Assuming You Know:** Even if you've heard it before, listen like it's new. Every customer's context is different.

Every one of these errors pushes the person further away; often without them being able to articulate why they feel disconnected. They just stop sharing. And when they stop sharing, you lose the ability to help them.

How to Practice Active Listening

1. **Record a Call or Conversation** — Play it back and measure how much you talked versus listened.
2. **Count the Links** — How many times did you use a Statement-Question combination?
3. **Track Discovery** — Did your follow-up questions reveal something deeper, or did they just circle back to features?
4. **Adjust** — Practice pausing two seconds after someone finishes speaking before replying. It resets your brain to listen mode.

This reflection builds awareness, and awareness sharpens skill. Some of the best salespeople I have coached were not naturally gifted talkers — they were extraordinary listeners. Listening is a learnable skill, and like any skill, it improves with intentional practice.

The Umbrella Game Connection

This is also why The Umbrella Game works so powerfully. Participants who "feature-dump" fail because they are focused on what they want to say instead of what the other person needs to hear. The game shows how easy it is to talk past people instead of listening to them. Listening reveals need, and need reveals opportunity. The customer who walked in asking *"Why do I need an umbrella?"* had the answer with them the entire time. They just needed someone to ask the right questions to bring it up.

PRO TIP: *After every customer interaction, ask yourself one question: "Did I learn at least three specific things about this customer that I did not know before the conversation started?" If you cannot answer yes, you were telling — not asking. Great listeners walk away from every conversation knowing more about the person than when they started. That knowledge becomes your next solution.*

Let's Review

- Active listening is the foundation of the Sales Linkage Process — everything else depends on it.
- **Turn the light on:** when you truly listen, customers will tell you everything you need. Stop guessing and start hearing.
- The Statement-Question Linked method validates the customer and advances the conversation simultaneously.
- Listening is not silence. It is active curiosity and genuine interest in what the other person is experiencing.
- Common mistakes like interrupting, assuming, and jumping to solutions are conversation killers. Avoid them deliberately.
- Practice by recording conversations, counting your "links," and measuring your talk-to-listen ratio.
- **Remember:** The more you listen, the less you have to sell. People guide themselves toward decisions when they feel truly understood.

Chapter 10: Crafting Urgency Statements

Turning Understanding into Action Without Pressure

Why Urgency Matters

Once a customer feels understood, the next step is helping them act before hesitation takes over. People often want the solution in front of them, but their natural tendency is to wait. Life gets in the way. Doubt creeps in. The clarity they felt in the moment starts to fade. Creating urgency is not about pushing harder. It is about protecting momentum. You earned trust through listening, and now you help the customer follow through on what they already know matters. When urgency is rooted in honesty and value, it becomes a service, not a tactic.

The Psychology of Delay

Behavioral economics tells us that people delay decisions for three main reasons:

1. **Loss Aversion** — Humans fear losing what they already have more than they enjoy gaining something new.

2. **Decision Fatigue** — The more choices people face, the more data they get, the more likely they are to stall. This is why marketing in a sale kills it.

3. **The Zeigarnik Effect** — Unfinished tasks linger in the mind, creating mental tension until resolved. Interestingly, this also means customers are relieved when they finalize a decision, even when they are hesitant going in.

Your role is to guide them gently toward resolution by connecting timing to benefit, not by forcing a deadline. When done right, urgency helps the customer close the mental loop on something they already wanted to do.

Four Healthy Sources of Urgency

1. **Scarcity (Reality, Not Drama):** *"Inventory on these colors moves quickly during event season, and I'd hate for you to miss your first choice."* Scarcity works when it's factual and framed as concern, not fear. Never invent scarcity. If it's not real, the customer will eventually find out — and the relationship will not survive it.

2. **Opportunity Cost:** *"Ordering this week locks in the current pricing before the new tariff takes effect."* This reframes waiting as losing value rather than spending more.

3. **Commitment Momentum:** *"You've already approved the artwork and confirmed quantities. The next step is simply confirming production, so we stay on schedule."* Progress itself creates motivation — remind them of it.

4. **Completion Relief:** *"Let's finalize this today so you can cross it off your list and focus on the event details."* Sometimes the best urgency is peace of mind.

Crafting the Statement

A strong urgency statement combines empathy, clarity, and purpose:

Step 1 — Acknowledge Understanding: *"I know staying on budget and timing are both priorities for you."*
Step 2 — Connect Benefit to Timing: *"If we move forward today, we can still meet your delivery window without rush fees."*

This is not persuasion. It is alignment. You are helping the customer act on their own best interest. You are not manufacturing urgency; you are surfacing it.

The Rhythm of Respectful Urgency

1. Listen First. Urgency without understanding sounds manipulative.
2. Confirm Value. Make sure they see what they are acting for, not what they are running from.
3. State Facts Clearly. No fluff, no exaggeration.
4. Invite Partnership. *"Let's get this in motion together."*

Common Pitfalls

- **False Deadlines:** They erode trust permanently. Never create urgency that does not exist.
- **Over-Explaining:** One clear statement beats three convincing paragraphs.
- **Emotional Hijacking:** Do not match a customer's anxiety; balance it with calm assurance.
- **Silence After the Statement:** Say it once, then let them respond. Trust the work you have done.

Real Examples

A nonprofit director once told me she needed mugs for a fundraiser *"sometime soon."* After linking needs and showing value, I said: *"Your event is on the 15th, and standard production is ten business days. If we approve today, delivery lands exactly two days before setup — that's perfect timing."* She replied, *"Let's do it now, so I can stop worrying about it."* That is the goal of healthy urgency, action through relief, not resistance.

Another example is insurance sales, many people believe they have plenty of time during Open Enrollment. The reality is that most people think the same way. It is like Christmas shopping: the longer people wait, the longer the lines become, and everyone begins calling at once. This overwhelms a system with a hard stop date and time, increases wait times, and forces customers to pause their lives longer than necessary just to secure protection. That is why sharing this with a customer is not pressure; it is practical and relevant guidance that helps them understand the benefit of acting sooner rather than later.

PRO TIP: *The most effective urgency statements are about the customer's timeline, not yours. "My month-end quota" is not a compelling reason for a customer to move fast. "Your event is in two weeks, and production takes ten days" is. Always anchor urgency to something the customer already told you was important. That is the difference between manipulation and genuine helpfulness.*

Let's Review

- Urgency is not manipulation. It is momentum with meaning.
- People delay because of loss aversion, decision fatigue, and the Zeigarnik effect. Your job is to help them resolve tension with confidence.
- Use the four healthy urgency sources: scarcity, opportunity cost, commitment momentum, and completion relief.
- Link urgency to benefit and timing — never to fear.
- Speak with empathy, clarity, and partnership — you are guiding, not pushing.
- Avoid false deadlines or emotional pressure. Authenticity builds trust.
- One calm, confident statement followed by silence is often enough.
- **Remember:** The best urgency ends with relief, not resistance.

Chapter 11: Chat, Text and SMS Selling

The Digital Messages Shift Is Real — Bringing the Human Touch to Digital Conversations

Technology has changed the way customers interact with businesses. Increasingly, first contact happens not on the phone or in person, but through chat windows, text messages, and direct messages. These conversations are fast-paced, customer-driven, and easy to abandon. It is the most impersonal way to communicate, which means it requires the most intentional effort to make it feel human. If you do not engage quickly and strategically, the opportunity disappears with a single click.

The Gen Z Shift Toward Digital Conversations

Generational shifts are reshaping sales communication. Gen Z, today's young adults, are the first generation to grow up entirely in a world of text, chat, and instant messaging. As they move into their 30s and become decision-makers in households and organizations, we can expect fewer phone calls and far more digital conversations. The winners will be the companies and salespeople who not only respond fast, but who also know how to link questions and solutions in real time over text and chat.

Pro research tip: If you have kids under 18 with phones, ask how often they use the voice feature. The answer is telling.

The **Sales Linkage Process** applies here just as it does on every other channel. The only difference is the speed and format. In chat and SMS, statements alone kill conversations. Every statement must be followed by a question to keep the customer engaged.

Why Speed and Engagement Matter

Research shows that 78% of customers buy from the company that responds to them first. In SMS and chat, people expect responses in seconds, not hours. If you take too long, they assume you are not interested, or worse, that you do not value their time.

Even more importantly, without engagement, the conversation dies. When you simply answer questions without asking one yourself, you risk two problems:

1. The customer gets the information they came for and leaves before discovering your solution.
2. You become nothing more than a Q&A agent, not a trusted sales professional.

Tone Travels Differently in Text

When customers cannot hear your voice or see your smile, tone has to live in your words. The best digital communicators convey warmth and competence in short bursts.

- Use short sentences. They're easier to digest on screens.
- Avoid all caps or long blocks of text. They feel overwhelming or aggressive.
- Add small relational cues. An *"!"* can replace a handshake when used sparingly.
- Use the customer's name. It personalizes the message even through a screen.

- Read their message twice before you respond. The words they choose reveal how they are feeling.

The goal is to sound human in a medium that often feels mechanical. A simple phrase like *"Sounds great, happy to help!"* reads friendlier than *"Ok."* Punctuation, spacing, and pacing all matter. Use them intentionally.

Statement-Question Linking in Chat

The same Statement-Question Linking principle we teach for live conversations is critical here.

Instead of: "Yes, we have that in stock."
Say: "Yes, we have that in stock. What's most important to you — fast delivery or the best price?"

The first statement ends the conversation. The second builds engagement and discovery, moving you deeper into the Sales Linkage Process.

Email and Professional Social Media Introductions

Email is still one of the most powerful sales tools in business, but too often it gets treated as a one-way marketing blast rather than a true sales conversation. Just like chat and SMS, emails must follow the Sales Linkage Process because your goal is not to dump data; it is to engage, uncover needs, and guide customers toward solutions.

Start With Attention and Relevance

The opening line of an email is everything. People decide in seconds whether to keep reading or delete. Instead of diving straight into your offer, begin with something personal, specific, and relevant. That might mean congratulating a business owner on a grand opening, mentioning a recent award they won, or referencing something about their business you researched:

"I really admire how active your company is in the community, and I'd love to support that mission by helping you with solutions that align with your goals."

Always Include a Call to Action

Every sales email should guide the customer to the next step. Ambiguity is the enemy. Instead of ending with *"Let me know,"* close with something specific:

- *"Does Thursday at 2 p.m. work for a quick conversation?"*
- *"Would you like me to send over a few examples of how we've helped other businesses like yours?"*

The Power of the P.S.

Never underestimate the power of a P.S. at the end of your email. Research in direct marketing shows the P.S. is one of the most-read lines in any letter or email. Use it as a hook or incentive (call to action): *"P.S. I'd be happy to extend a 10% discount for first-time orders placed this month."* That one extra line can re-engage readers who skimmed and spark action.

A Personal Example

I once had a customer reach out over chat asking if a promotional product came in bulk pricing. Instead of answering *"yes"* and ending the conversation, I asked: *"Yes, it does. What event are you planning for?"* That one question led to uncovering a corporate conference with 800 attendees. What could have been a quick one-off order turned into a long-term account worth six figures because I linked a statement with a question.

When to Escalate Beyond Chat

Chat and text are excellent for speed, but not for depth. If the conversation grows too detailed, or you sense the customer's needs are complex, offer to move the conversation to a call or in-person meeting: *"That's a great question, and there are a couple of options depending on your situation. Would it be easier if we set up a quick 10-minute call so I can walk you through them?"*

If a call is not possible, keep engagement alive by asking discovery questions. Questions extend conversations; statements end them.

Sales Leader Callout

Leaders must train their teams that chat and text are not customer service tools only; they are sales tools. Coach your reps to:

- Respond quickly — within 60 seconds if possible.
- Always follow a statement with a question.
- Transition to calls or meetings when depth is needed.
- Track conversions from chat to sale, just as you would for phone calls.
- Never let a digital conversation end without a clear next step.

PRO TIP: *Read the customer's punctuation. "Need these fast!!!" signals stress and a history of being let down. Responding with, "Got it — we'll make sure timing works perfectly. Let me confirm a few details so we can deliver on that," turns a tense customer into a relieved one before you have even confirmed the order. Written listening is a skill. Practice it.*

Let's Review

- Digital communication is today's first handshake — warmth and speed matter most.
- Tone lives in punctuation, phrasing, and pacing. Use them to sound human.
- Apply Statement-Question Linking to show understanding in text.
- Keep every message short, clear, and forward-moving.
- Respond fast — even a simple acknowledgment builds trust.
- Emails need a personal opening, a clear call to action, and a strong P.S.
- Never let a digital conversation end without a clear next step.
- **Key Reminder:** The difference between a "support agent" and a "sales professional" in chat comes down to one habit — always link statements with questions.

Chapter 12: The Umbrella Game — Why Do I Need an Umbrella?

Applying the Sales Linkage Process

You've seen how the Sales Linkage Process adapts to every channel. Now it's time to see where it all began. The Umbrella Game is more than a teaching tool; it's the moment you realize how easily we talk past customers when we forget to listen.

The Umbrella Game is an engaging and dynamic approach to practicing how to uncover customer needs, link solutions, and sharpen your overall sales skills. By placing sales professionals in real-world scenarios and asking them to step outside their usual product or service offerings, this game challenges participants to think creatively and cultivate the expertise necessary to connect with customers, address their concerns, and close deals successfully.

Why Umbrellas?

Simply put, umbrellas are universally understood. When you hand a salesperson an umbrella, they instantly transform into marketers. They know exactly what it does, how it works, and how to talk about it. Everyone has experience with umbrellas, which is precisely the problem. **Familiarity breeds assumption, and assumption is the enemy of discovery.**

Marketing vs. Sales

When you look up the definition of sales, it's no wonder there's confusion. Many definitions mention trading money for services or products, or even discounting goods; but they don't capture what we, as sales professionals, do. Our role goes beyond completing transactions; it's about engaging customers by asking questions to identify their needs, offering solutions that address those needs, and ensuring alignment by checking for agreement.

Marketing, on the other hand, tells. It's designed to get the phone to ring, build awareness, and draw people into locations or prompt them to purchase. Once marketing has done its job, it's time for sales to step in and ask the right questions to uncover deeper needs.

Remember: Marketing tells, sales asks. If we're telling, we're not selling.

Why Do I Need an Umbrella?

Imagine a customer walking into a store and asking, *"Why do I need an umbrella?"* Many salespeople instinctively jump into feature-dumping mode: *"It protects you from rain!"* or *"It's lightweight and easy to carry!"* While these points may be true, they miss the heart of the question. The real answer lies in understanding the customer's needs. Why do they need an umbrella? Is it for rain, sun, or something else entirely? The only way to find out is by asking the right questions.

Without realizing it, in an automatic reaction, people often start blurting out things they believe umbrellas do. What they forget is that a customer is standing right in front of them and they have not yet uncovered why this customer truly needs an umbrella.

The Story

I start the Umbrella Game by telling the class they've been given an umbrella store to run. I walk in as a customer and ask, *"Why do I need an umbrella?"* Immediately, I get marketing-style answers: *"It protects you from rain," "It's durable,"* or *"It's great for all seasons."* I stop them and say, *"This is a great ad campaign! But… WHY DO I NEED ONE?"*

This question keeps going around the room until, finally, someone says, *"I don't know… why do you need one?"* That's when I tell them my story:

"I came home the other day, and I saw my kids playing with water guns in the backyard. I really enjoy when they're outside having fun. But one of my little angels decided to grab my golf umbrella and use it as a shield. They bashed that thing on the shed, the brick wall, and the pool. Now, I don't want to discourage them from being creative and having fun, but I also don't want my stuff to get abused in the process. So today, I'm here to buy one umbrella for each of my kids in their favorite color. I also need to replace the golf umbrella they wrecked."

I then look around at the students and ask, *"How many of you guessed that?"* Nobody ever does. And that's the point. The answer was in front of them the entire time. In the very question I asked. *"Why do I need an umbrella?"* was in fact the question they should have been asking me.

The point here is to allow mistakes without saying "wrong" or chastising anyone. This is about learning. We want people to have that "Ah-ha!" moment when they realize how much more effective it is to ask the right questions and uncover the real reasons behind the customer's needs.

The Rules of the Umbrella Game

1. Start with the question: When a customer walks in and asks, *"Why do I need an umbrella?"* — don't over-explain or elaborate. Simply answer with a question to better understand their needs.

2. Allow the conversation to unfold naturally: Let the participants guess different answers based on the features of the umbrella. This is where they learn what doesn't work.

3. Avoid giving the answer too quickly: Let the game play out until someone asks, *"I don't know, why do you need one?"* Then share your story.

4. Foster reflection and discussion: After the game, reflect on the experience. Ask participants if they were in "marketing" mode or "sales" mode.

5. Allow mistakes without judgment: The goal is to learn from experience, not to correct in the moment.

The Lesson of the Umbrella Game

Focus on the customer's needs, not the product's features. When you prioritize discovery and understanding, the solution becomes obvious, and the customer feels confident in their decision. Remember: Sales asks.

Real-World Applications

- **Insurance Sales:** Instead of pitching a plan right away, ask, *"What's most important to you in a policy?"*
- **Technology Sales:** Focus on the customer's workflow with, *"What's your biggest challenge with your current system?"*
- **Retail Sales:** Discover the customer's priorities with, *"How do you plan to use this in your daily life?"*

PRO TIP: *Use The Umbrella Game in your next team meeting or training session. Give every person on your team an umbrella — real or imaginary — and walk in as the customer. You will immediately see which of your team members are marketers and which are salespeople. Then coach them toward the right questions. The game takes ten minutes and teaches more about needs discovery than most full-day training programs.*

Let's Review

- The Umbrella Game exposes how naturally we jump to features before we understand needs.
- Marketing tells, sales asks — this is the central lesson of the game.
- The answer is always in front of you — you just have to ask the right question to surface it.
- Allow mistakes in training. The "Ah-ha!" moment cannot be forced, only created through experience.
- The same principle applies in every industry and every sales environment.
- **Remember:** If you are telling, you are not selling. Sales asks.

Chapter 13: The Power of Follow-Up

Turning Transactions into Relationships

The Bridge Between Close and Continuity

The sale does not end when the contract is signed or the product is delivered. In fact, one of the most critical, and most overlooked, steps in the entire sales process is what happens *after* closing. Follow-up is where transactions become trust, and trust becomes loyalty.

Staying on offense does not end when the first conversation does. Momentum means nothing without follow-through. The best salespeople do not wait for opportunities to reopen; they create them through purposeful, consistent follow-up.

Think of it this way: you planted a seed during the sale. Follow-up is the water. Without it, the seed dies before anything grows.

Why Follow-Up Gets Skipped

Most salespeople know they should follow up. They simply do not. Here is why and why that mindset must change:

- **Fear of being annoying.** Reframe this completely. Follow-up is not an interruption; it is an investment. When it delivers value, customers welcome it.
- **Assuming the sale is done.** The close is not the end of the relationship. It is the beginning of it. Every sale you close is the start of a long-term conversation.
- **No system.** Without a follow-up system, good intentions fade. We will discuss tools shortly.

The data tells a stark story: research from the Brevet Group shows that 80% of sales require at least five follow-ups to close, yet 44% of salespeople give up after just one. That gap is your competitive advantage.

Benefits of Effective Follow-Up

Strengthens the Relationship: Customers remember salespeople who make them feel valued after the transaction, not just during it. A simple check-in says, *"You mattered to me before the sale, and you still do."*

Uncovers Additional Needs: As customers use your product or service, new needs emerge. Following up creates the space to discover them before they take their business elsewhere.

Drives Referrals: Satisfied, well-followed customers are your most powerful marketing channel. They do not just buy again, they send others. Research shows that referrals from existing customers close at a dramatically higher rate than cold outreach.

Improves Retention: Regular follow-ups reduce churn by ensuring customers remain satisfied, heard, and engaged. People do not leave vendors they feel genuinely connected to.

A Follow-Up Framework That Works

Step 1 — Within 24 to 48 Hours of the Sale: Send a genuine thank-you. Not automated. Not generic. Personal.

"Thank you for trusting me to help you with [specific solution]. I am genuinely excited to see the positive impact this will have on you. Please reach out any time — I am here."

Promptness signals respect. A quick response shows attentiveness, and that first message after the sale sets the tone for the entire relationship going forward.

Step 2 — Shortly After Delivery: Check in once the product or service is in the customer's hands. Confirm satisfaction, address any issues, and open the door to feedback.

"I wanted to check in and see how things are going with [product/service]. Is there anything I can help with or improve?"

Step 3 — Periodically Over Time: Schedule regular check-ins; quarterly, seasonally, or annually depending on your industry. Use these opportunities to share relevant updates, new solutions, or simply to reconnect as a human being.

"It has been a few months since we last connected. I wanted to check in and see how things are going. Are there any new challenges I can help you solve?"

How to Make Follow-Ups Meaningful

Generic follow-ups feel transactional. Personalized ones feel intentional. The difference is in the details: the customer's name, their event date, the color they mentioned, the challenge they shared. Those small specifics tell the customer that you were paying attention, and that you still are.

Use what you learned during active listening. Reference specific things the customer told you; their event date, their color preferences, the challenge they mentioned, the goal they shared. That level of recall is not just professional; it is powerful.

"You mentioned wanting these in time for your volunteer banquet, production is on track for delivery by Thursday."

That one sentence proves you listened. It builds loyalty faster than any discount ever could.

Add Value, Not Just Check-Ins: Every follow-up should move the relationship forward or remove friction. Replace "just following up" with something that actually serves:

- *"Wanted to share an idea that could complement your last order."*
- *"Here is a quick update on delivery — we are right on track."*
- *"I came across this article and thought of you immediately."*

You are not checking a box. You are deepening a partnership.

Mix Your Methods:

Different customers prefer different channels:

- **Phone:** Best for relationship updates, complex issues, or high-stakes conversations.
- **Direct Mail:** A great way to change it up and still a reliable channel. Expect slower response times.
- **Email:** Perfect for confirmations, visual proofs, and next-step summaries.
- **Text/Chat:** Ideal for quick check-ins and fast responses.

The key is variety with intention. Never send three messages that all say the same thing. Each contact should add something new: clarity, reassurance, or value.

Tools That Support Great Follow-Up

- **CRM Systems:** Track every interaction, set reminders, and never let a follow-up fall through the cracks.
- **Email Templates:** Build personalized templates for common scenarios so follow-up stays fast without losing the human touch.
- **Calendar Blocking:** Protect follow-up time on your calendar the same way you protect meetings.
- **AI Drafting Tools:** Use them to help with wording when you are stuck but always add your personal voice before sending. Proof it all!

A follow-up system does not make you robotic. It makes you reliable. And reliability is the foundation of trust.

The Follow-Through Loop

Think of follow-up as a loop, not a list:

After Delivery: Send a genuine thank-you and confirm satisfaction. *"How did everything turn out? Anything you'd want to tweak next time?"*

After a Positive Response: Add value. *"Since you loved those tumblers, want to see matching tote options for your next event?"*

After a Pause: Stay visible without being intrusive. *"Thought of you when this new line launched — it fits your brand perfectly."*

Each touchpoint builds emotional equity. You are not just checking in; you are staying invested.

People often say, "Go the extra mile." I agree because there is far less competition there. Most salespeople stop at the first or second contact, leaving a massive opportunity for those willing to stay in the conversation. If you will not take care of them, your competitor will.

PRO TIP: *The single most effective follow-up habit is writing down one specific thing from every customer conversation — a detail, a goal, a worry they mentioned. Then reference it in your next touchpoint. That one practice separates the professionals who get referrals from the ones who keep cold-calling strangers. The customer who said "we're planning a big event in the fall" is your next major order. But only if you remembered they said it.*

Let's Review

- Follow-up is not optional. It is the difference between a transaction and a lasting relationship.
- 80% of sales require five or more follow-ups. Most salespeople stop after one. That gap is your advantage.
- Timely, personalized follow-ups strengthen trust, uncover new needs, and drive referrals.
- Replace generic check-ins with messages that add genuine value — reference what you learned, not just what you sold.
- Use a system: CRM reminders, calendar blocks, and templates keep follow-up consistent without killing creativity.
- Vary your channels — phone, email, and text each have their place.
- **Remember:** Follow-through is offense in motion. Every touchpoint is a link in the chain of a lasting relationship.

Chapter 14: Navigating Objections — Turning Hesitation into Understanding

How to Keep the Conversation Moving Forward with Confidence and Care

Objections Are Not Rejections

Here is the truth most sales training gets wrong: objections are not obstacles to the sale; they are invitations to go deeper. When a customer objects, they are not saying no. They are saying, *"I am not yet sure enough to say yes."* That is an entirely different situation, and it requires an entirely different response.

The best salespeople in the world do not overcome objections. They *understand* them. There is a meaningful difference. Overcoming implies a battle, one side wins, one side loses. Understanding implies partnership and both sides work toward the same goal.

When hesitation appears, your first instinct should be curiosity, not correction.

Why People Object

Every objection comes from one of three places:

- **Uncertainty** — They do not yet trust the outcome. They need more confidence in what they are buying and who they are buying it from.
- **Information Gaps** — They do not see how the details connect to their specific situation. The value has not been made real enough for them yet.

- **Perceived Risk** — They fear loss more than they anticipate gain. This is loss aversion at work — a well-documented psychological tendency to weigh potential losses more heavily than equivalent gains.

Recognizing which type you are dealing with keeps you proactive. Remember what you learned in Active Listening: objections are often emotions wearing logical masks. Listen for what they *mean*, not just what they *say*.

The Right Sequence: Validate, Then Clarify

The instinct under pressure is to explain immediately — to defend, justify, and prove. Resist that. Before offering any information, acknowledge the emotion behind the objection. Validation opens doors that logic alone cannot.

"I completely understand why you would want to double-check that." "That is a smart concern — I would be asking the same thing in your position."

That acknowledgment does something remarkable: it diffuses tension instantly. Once the customer feels truly heard, they can actually hear you. Until then, anything you say just sounds like a salesperson pushing back.

Then — and only then — move into clarification or value reinforcement:

"Here is how this option actually prevents that concern." "That is exactly why we designed it this way — so you do not have to worry about that later."

Validate first. Explain second. That is offense in empathy form.

Common Objections and How to Handle Them

"That's too expensive." This is the most common objection in sales — and it almost never means what it sounds like. It usually means, *"I do not yet see the value clearly enough."*

"That makes complete sense. Let me connect this back to what you told me was most important... [restate their need]. When you factor in [specific benefit], the cost per [day/use/outcome] actually works out to [number]. Does that change how you're looking at it?"

"I need to think about it." This is rarely about thinking. It is almost always about uncertainty — a specific concern they have not voiced yet.

"Of course — I want you to feel completely comfortable. Can I ask, is there a specific part you are still unsure about? I would rather address that now than have you leave with a question I could have answered."

"I can get this cheaper somewhere else." Do not argue. Acknowledge it and pivot to value.

"You absolutely can, and I want to make sure you are comparing the same thing. The option you are referencing does not include [specific feature you mentioned was important to them]. When you factor in [replacement cost / quality / timeline], this actually saves you money over time. Can I show you the math on that?"

"It is not in the budget right now." *"I understand — budgets are tight for a lot of teams right now. Let me ask: when would be a better time? And in the meantime, would it help if I showed you a scaled-down option that delivers the core of what you need without the full investment?"* Always keep the door open.

"I need to talk to my spouse / partner / boss." *"That makes total sense — big decisions are better made together. Can I ask, what do you think their biggest* *concern might be? If we can address that now, you will walk into that conversation with all the answers."*

"I had a bad experience with a similar product before." This is an emotional objection. Validate first, always. *"I am sorry that happened — that is genuinely frustrating. Can you tell me a little about what went wrong? I want to make sure what we are looking at here solves exactly that problem, not just replaces it."*

"I'm happy with what I have now." *"That is great to hear. A lot of our best customers said the same thing before they found out [specific advantage]. Not saying this is a fit for you — but would you mind if I shared one thing that might change how you see it? It will only take a minute."*

Bridging Back to Value

Every objection is an invitation to reconnect the conversation to what the customer already told you mattered most. When they hesitate about price, timing, or a feature, go back to their words and thoughts.

"You mentioned earlier that reliability was your biggest priority. That is exactly what this addresses." "Earlier you said quality control was key. This approach keeps that standard intact."

This is not defending your product. It *reminds* them why they were interested in the first place. You are linking their priorities to your solution so they can rediscover why it fits, in their own words.

When the Answer Is "Not Yet"

Sometimes the honest answer is that the timing is simply not right. Staying on offense does not mean forcing a decision; it means keeping the relationship alive.

"I will send you a quick summary of what we discussed, and I will check back closer to your next event to see if the timing feels better then."

That one statement does three things: it demonstrates respect, reinforces reliability, and signals ongoing partnership. You are not chasing; you are continuing.

The Psychology Behind Hesitation

Two powerful forces fuel most objections:

Cognitive Dissonance: The mental discomfort between wanting something and fearing the decision. This is the internal friction of change.

Loss Aversion: The deep-wired human instinct to avoid potential loss, even when the gain clearly outweighs it. Psychologists Daniel Kahneman and Amos Tversky showed that losses feel roughly twice as painful as equivalent gains feel pleasurable. Acknowledging this reality and gently helping customers see what they are *losing* by not moving forward, can shift the balance.

Your job is not to eliminate these feelings. It is to balance them with empathy, transparency, and reassurance. When people feel emotionally safe, they make decisions on their own.

PRO TIP: *Write down the five objections you hear most often in your specific role. For each one, script two responses — one for uncertainty and one for a genuine information gap. Then practice them out loud until they sound completely natural, not rehearsed. When an objection arrives in a live conversation, you will not be scrambling. You will be ready. The difference between a salesperson who panics at pushback and one who handles it smoothly is almost never talent. It is preparation.*

Let's Review

- Objections are not rejections — they are requests for more information, clarity, or reassurance.
- Every objection comes from uncertainty, an information gap, or perceived risk. Identify which before responding.
- Validate the emotion before you offer logic. People cannot hear you until they feel heard.
- Use the Statement-Question Linked method: acknowledge, then ask what is really behind the concern.
- Bridge every objection back to the customer's original stated needs — use their own words.
- Prepare scripted responses for your five most common objections. Practice them until they are natural.
- When the timing is simply not right, keep the door open gracefully. A "not yet" is not a "no."

- **Remember:** The goal is not to overcome objections. It is to understand them. One leads to pressure, the other leads to partnership.

Chapter 15: Building Lifelong Relationships Through Sales

From One-Time Transactions to Trusted Partnerships

The Bridge from Hesitation to Connection

Once you have navigated objections with empathy and understanding, the natural next step is to nurture the relationship you have earned. Every conversation, whether it ends in an immediate order or a graceful "not yet" plants a seed. The long-term health of your business depends entirely on what you do with it after it is planted.

Relationships are where transactions mature into trust, and trust becomes loyalty. Numbers measure sales performance. Relationships measure *career* performance.

Why Relationships Are Real Business

In today's marketplace, customers have more options than ever. What separates great salespeople from good ones is not product knowledge or closing technique. It is the depth of connection they build with the people they serve.

A single sale makes your day. A relationship builds your future.

When customers genuinely trust you:

- They stay loyal even when a competitor offers a lower price.
- They refer their friends, colleagues, and family — the highest form of validation.
- They tell you the truth about their concerns, which makes your job infinitely easier.

- They forgive mistakes, because the relationship has a balance large enough to absorb them.

Research by Redpoint Global found that 74% of consumers stay with a company because they feel understood and valued. That is a relationship outcome, not a product outcome. You cannot manufacture that with a promotion or sale.

The Foundations of Relationship Selling

Consistency: Show up the same way every time, professional, reliable, and kind. Consistency is credibility in motion. Customers do not need you to be perfect; they need to be able to predict you. When they know what to expect from you, they stop looking elsewhere.

Memory: Remember details. The customer who mentioned their daughter's college graduation, the one who said their logo color was very specific, the one who was nervous about their first big event; reference those things later. It shows they mattered to you beyond the transaction.

Transparency: Honesty builds speed. When problems arise, they will, own them early and clearly. A sincere apology delivered quickly can deepen trust more than avoiding errors altogether. People remember integrity longer than they remember inconvenience.

Recognition: Celebrate milestones. A quick "Congratulations on your 10-year anniversary!" note or a small discount on a milestone order creates goodwill that marketing cannot replicate. Small gestures carry compound interest.

Reciprocity: When you give value, information, time, insight, genuine care, people instinctively want to give back through loyalty and referrals. You do not have to ask for it. You just have to earn it.

Principles for Building Lifelong Relationships

Show Genuine Care: Customers can feel the difference between someone going through the motions and someone who is genuinely invested in their success. They made the distinction before they even knew they were making it.

Instead of: *"Let me know if you need anything."* Try: *"I have been thinking about your situation and found something that might make things easier for you."*

One of those closes a door. The other opens one.

Focus on Long-Term Value: Not every recommendation should be the most expensive option. Sometimes the right move is to recommend something smaller, simpler, or more appropriate, even if it means a smaller commission today. That kind of integrity is noticed. It is remembered. And it comes back to you many times over.

Become a Trusted Advisor: The highest form of a sales relationship is when the customer calls you before they have a need, not after. When they ask, *"What do you think I should do here?"* you have stopped being a vendor and become a partner. That position is earned through consistent honesty, genuine expertise, and a track record of doing what you say you will do.

Personalize Every Interaction: Customers remember salespeople who treat them as individuals, not as accounts. Use their name. Reference past conversations. Acknowledge their specific situation. Never make them feel like you forgot everything they told you the last time.

"Last time we spoke, you mentioned you were focused on cutting costs. How has that been going?"

That one question says more about your character than any brochure or pitch ever could.

Turning Customers into Advocates

Happy customers are not just repeat buyers, they will become your most powerful sales force. Social proof is a real thing and word of mouth is the founding member of social proof. Here is how to turn a satisfied customer into someone who genuinely advocates for your brand:

- **Deliver more than expected.** Slightly exceed the promise. Arrive early. Deliver ahead of schedule. Throw in something small and unexpected.
- **Ask for feedback genuinely.** Not just a survey — a real conversation. *"Is there anything I could have done better for you?"*
- **Ask for referrals at the right moment.** Immediately after a positive interaction is the ideal time. *"I am so glad this worked out for you. If you know anyone facing a similar challenge, I would love to help them too."*
- **Follow up after referrals.** If a customer sends you a lead, close that loop. *"I wanted to let you know I spoke with your colleague — thank you for thinking of me."*

The Relationship Loop

Think of relationships as loops, not ladders. Each interaction cycles back into another:

Listen → Serve → Deliver → Follow Through → Reconnect

The loop never ends; it evolves. Some loops span a single season; others span entire careers. Staying on offense here means never assuming the relationship is fully established. You earn it again, quietly, every time you communicate.

When Things Go Wrong

Even in the strongest relationships, mistakes happen. An order arrives late. The wrong color shows up. Something gets missed. The measure of a professional is not whether these things happen. It is how you respond when they do.

A fast, honest response recovers more trust than the perfect delivery ever built. Own the mistake completely:

"You are right, and I am sorry. Here is what happened, what we are doing to fix it, and what we will do differently going forward."

That kind of accountability transforms a negative experience into a story the customer talks about *how well you handled it* — not about the mistake itself.

Building Relationships Inside Your Organization

Strong customer relationships do not happen in isolation. They are supported by equally strong internal relationships between sales, customer care, and operations. When your organization communicates openly and follows through on internal commitments, customers feel it.

The same listening, validation, and follow-through that build external trust apply internally too. Great sales cultures are built from the inside out.

The Role of Gratitude

Gratitude is one of the most underused tools in all of sales. A genuine, personal, timely thank-you creates emotional connection that no marketing campaign can manufacture.

"I appreciate the trust you place in me every time you order."

That sentence costs nothing and builds everything. Gratitude closes emotional distance. It reminds the customer that behind the emails and invoices is a human being who genuinely cares about their success.

PRO TIP: *A study analyzing 350,000 emails found that those ending with expressions of genuine gratitude — like "Thanks in advance for your time" — generated a response rate of 65.7%, compared to 46% for emails without a warm closing. That is not a small difference. The same principle applies to every form of communication. End with something that leaves the person feeling valued, not just informed. Every interaction is either adding to the relationship or drawing it down. Gratitude is always a deposit.*

Let's Review

- Relationships are the real measure of sales success — numbers measure performance, but relationships measure careers.
- Consistency, memory, transparency, recognition, and reciprocity are the foundations of lasting trust.
- Genuine care is not a tactic. It is a posture. Customers feel the difference.
- Become a trusted advisor by prioritizing the customer's best interest, even when it costs you something in the short term.
- Personalize every interaction by referencing specific things you learned about each customer.
- Turn satisfied customers into advocates by exceeding expectations and asking for referrals at the right moment.
- Handle mistakes quickly, honestly, and completely. Recovery builds more trust than perfection.
- **Remember:** Every conversation is either adding to the relationship or drawing from it. Gratitude, follow-through, and genuine care are always deposits.

Chapter 16: The Art of Sales Leadership

Inspiring and Guiding the Next Generation of Solutionists

Leadership Is the Long Game

Strong relationships do not stop with customers; they extend to the people we lead. The same empathy, listening, and follow-through that win customer's trust also build teams. When I coach, I coach like I sell: I ask questions that lead people to self-discovery rather than telling them what to think. A good leader does not create just followers; they create other leaders.

Sales leadership is not about authority or title. It is about influence. Great leaders create environments where confidence, creativity, and accountability thrive, not because they demand it, but because they model it.

What Makes a Great Sales Leader

Great sales leadership is a specific combination of technical skill, emotional intelligence, and an unwavering commitment to the growth of the people on your team. Here are the traits that separate great leaders from well-intentioned managers:

They inspect what they expect. You cannot coach from assumption. If you believe your team knows how to handle an objection, the only way to verify that is to put them in a situation where you can observe it. A coaching session without a demonstrated skill is just a conversation. Go watch. Go listen. Show up unannounced. The data you collect in the field is far more valuable than any report.

They coach early — before failure, not after. Too many leaders confuse coaching with correction. Real coaching happens *before* the missed QA score, *before* the lost deal, *before* the customer complaint. Reactive coaching is damage control. Proactive coaching is development. The goal is to prepare your team for the hard conversations and tough objections before those moments arrive in real time.

They over-communicate. Silence in leadership breeds confusion. When your team does not know what to expect, they fill the gap with anxiety. Over-communicate expectations, changes, recognition, and feedback. Repeat what matters. Say it different ways. Then say it again. Clarity is a gift, give it generously.

They lead one-on-one. The most powerful coaching tool in any leader's toolkit is consistent, structured one-on-one time with each team member. Not group meetings. Not broadcast emails. Individual conversations where the focus is entirely on that person's growth, challenges, and goals. When people feel seen individually, they perform differently.

They use roleplay as a development tool. Just as we would never send a football team onto the field without practicing the plays, we should never send salespeople into live conversations without rehearsing the difficult moments. Roleplay is not practice for beginners. It is the professional standard. Great teams drill objections, practice commitment scripts, and refine their approach in a safe environment before they need to execute under pressure.

They ask self-identifying questions. The most effective coaching does not tell people what they did wrong — it guides them to discover it themselves. *"Walk me through that conversation. Where do you think you could have taken a different approach?"* Self-discovery creates ownership.

Ownership creates change. Telling creates compliance and compliance disappears when you are not watching.

The Skill vs. Will Framework

I have often heard it said that coaching comes down to either skill or will — either the person does not know how, or they do not want to. In my experience, this framing misses something important.

If we focus only on criticizing behavior without equipping people with the skills to change it, we diminish their motivation. But when we build a coaching environment that genuinely develops skills, the will to excel follows naturally. I liken this to learning to roller skate. When you first started, you fell constantly. But with persistence, and especially with guidance from someone who could show you how, you improved quickly. Once you master it, you *want* to keep going. You were not just compliant; you were excited.

The same is true for your sales team. Build the skill, and the will shows up on its own.

The One-on-One Cadence

Structured one-on-one sessions are the backbone of a high-performing sales culture. Here is a simple framework for making them effective:

1. **Start by asking how they are doing** — genuinely, before anything else. The answer to that question shapes everything that follows.

2. **Review one skill at a time.** Just as in sales, where we focus on one need and one solution, coaching addresses one development gap at a time. Trying to fix everything at once fixes nothing.

3. **Ask before telling.** *"How do you think that went?"* before you share your perspective. Nine times out of ten, they already know what went wrong — they just need permission to say it.

4. **Articulate the skill clearly.** Make sure they can say exactly what they are going to do differently, not just agree that something should change. Vague coaching produces vague improvement.

5. **Follow through.** Go back and observe. Did they apply what you discussed? Coaching without follow-up is just talking.

Building a High-Performing Sales Culture

Invest in Training and Development: A well-trained team is a confident team. Provide ongoing learning opportunities, workshops, role plays, peer interviews, and access to the tools they need to grow. The Sales Linkage Process is straightforward to teach because it follows a clear, logical sequence. Your job is to ensure each person can not only follow the steps but articulate them fluently, in their own words, in any conversation.

Coach Early and Often: Do not wait for problems to surface. Build a regular cadence of coaching sessions, observations, and feedback loops. The team that practices hardest is almost never the most talented one. It is the most prepared one.

Celebrate Wins — Big and Small: Recognition is a multiplier. Publicly celebrating good behavior reinforces exactly the actions you want repeated. Create a "Wins Wall" where team members can share their successes. Post team stats openly. Recognize specific behaviors, not just outcomes.

"What I noticed you did in that conversation was outstanding; you stayed completely calm when they pushed back on price, and you brought them right back to their own words. That is Sales Linkage in action."

Specific recognition is far more powerful than general praise. *"Great job"* fades. *"Here is exactly what you did well and why it worked"* stays with people.

Encourage Collaboration: Sales can feel like an individual sport. Make it a team one. Have your top performers share their best lines, their most effective objection-handling techniques, and their wins in open forum. One person's breakthrough becomes the whole team's tool.

Inspire Through Purpose: Quotas are not motivating long-term. Purpose is. Help your team understand the *why* behind their work, the customers they genuinely helped, the problems they solved, the lives they made easier. Share those stories often. Remind them that being a solutionist is not about making a sale; it is about making a difference. I can not wait to share with you af2coaching.com that will help you coach and develop.

Leadership Is Not Promotion — It Is Multiplication

When your team wins, it is because they trusted your direction. When your customers stay, it is because they feel your team's consistency through every interaction. Your job as a leader is not to be the best salesperson in the room. It is to make everyone else better.

Leadership is multiplication. Every skill you develop in someone else grows your impact beyond what you could ever achieve alone.

I plan to expand on these principles in a dedicated coaching and leadership book, which will outline effective one-on-one strategies, the concept of triad coaching for enhanced team support, and a proven framework for building cultures of accountability and growth. But this is the foundation: coach like you sell, inspect what you expect, over-communicate with intention, and invest in your people like they are your most valuable product because they are.

PRO TIP: *85% of your time as a sales leader should be spent coaching — not in meetings, not doing admin, not filling out reports. Coaching. That means live call observations, structured one-on-ones, roleplay sessions, and ride-alongs. If your schedule does not reflect that, your culture will. Leaders shape what they invest in. Invest in your people, and your people will invest in your customers. The math is that simple — and that is important.*

What to learn more: af2coaching.com

Let's Review

- Great sales leaders inspire trust, collaboration, and growth — not through authority, but through influence and modeling.
- **Inspect what you expect:** coaching without observation is just conversation.
- **Over-communicate:** clarity is a gift. Give it generously and repeatedly.
- **Coach one-on-one:** individual attention changes performance in ways group meetings never can.
- Use self-identifying questions to guide people toward their own discoveries — self-discovery creates ownership.
- Address skill gaps first. When the skill is there, the will follows naturally.
- Use roleplay to prepare your team *before* they face hard moments in live conversations.
- Celebrate specific behaviors publicly — recognition that names what was done right gets repeated.
- **Remember:** Leadership is multiplication. The best leaders make everyone around them better. That is the only metric that truly matters.

Chapter 17: Other Helpful Hints — Tools, Habits, and Tips for Everyday Success

Putting the Sales Linkage Process to Work in Every Situation

Why This Chapter Exists

By now, you have mastered the mindset, the process, and the psychology behind the Sales Linkage approach. You have learned how to connect, understand, serve, follow through, lead, and build relationships that last. But real-world success also depends on the habits, tools, and daily adjustments that keep you consistent across every environment.

This chapter collects the most practical tips, methods, and reminders to help you apply the Sales Linkage Process wherever you go — in any industry, on any platform, with any customer.

Time and Task Management: Protecting the Minutes That Build Legacy

Sales is not about working longer. It is about working smarter and more intentionally. Time is the one resource you cannot recover, which means protecting the right hours is itself a sales strategy.

The Daily Power of 3

Each day, commit to three types of focused activity:

- **3 Conversations to Open:** Reach out proactively to new or dormant contacts.
- **3 Follow-Throughs:** Revisit prior customers or pending conversations with something of value.

- **3 Improvements:** One personal, one process-related, one product or industry insight learned.

Nine focused actions compounded daily produce remarkable momentum over a year.

Batch Administrative Work — Protect Relational Time

Handle email, quotes, and admin in grouped blocks so you can be fully present in your customer conversations. Multitasking fractures attention and erodes trust. When you are with a customer, be *with* them — entirely. The phone stays away. The email tab stays closed. Attention is the purest form of respect.

Use Technology to Track, Not to Distract

CRM systems, reminders, and dashboards are tools for insight — not replacements for human connection. Let them record your promises so your brain is free to focus on people. If you are ever stuck drafting an email or stuck on wording, do not waste time staring at a blank screen. Use an AI tool to get the words flowing and then make it yours. Do not let administrative friction slow you down or hurt your value is in the conversations.

Networking and Referrals: Multiplying Your Reach

Referrals are the highest form of trust. They mean your reputation is speaking for you before you even enter the room.

Give Before You Request

Share useful ideas, connect people with each other, recommend contacts without expecting anything in return. Reach out and ask, *'How can I help you promote your products or services?"* Do not wait for them to ask. When you give freely and consistently, people naturally want to give back.

Ask at the Right Moment

The best time to ask for a referral is immediately after a positive interaction or successful delivery — when the customer is at peak satisfaction:

"I am so glad this worked out well for you. If you know anyone facing a similar challenge, I would love to help them too."

Or even more direct:

"It has been a pleasure to assist you today, Mr. Johnson. Is there anyone else you know who could use the same kind of help?"

Stay Visible Between Sales

Networking is not just collecting contacts. It is staying remembered. Use quick check-ins, social updates, or brief notes of encouragement to keep your name associated with value. When you reach out between transactions just to say hello, it removes the "using them" vibe from every future outreach.

The Referral Loop

- Deliver an exceptional experience.
- Ask for an introduction.
- Acknowledge the referral with genuine gratitude.
- Report back when it becomes a success.

This simple cycle deepens loyalty on both sides. And when a customer is willing, ask them to leave a review or share their experience publicly — that kind of endorsement extends your reach far beyond your personal network.

Conversation Openers: Expanding Your Library

Even seasoned professionals occasionally face the blank screen moment when starting a new outreach. Here are natural, human-centered openers that follow the Sales Linkage principles:

Warm Outreach (Existing or Referred Contact) *"Hey [Name], I just finished a project similar to yours and thought you'd appreciate seeing how it turned out. Mind if I share the idea with you?"*

Cold Outreach (No Prior Contact) *"Hi [Name], I noticed your company is doing [context]. We have helped similar teams with [specific challenge]. Would it make sense to compare notes?"*

Re-Engagement (Past Contact Who Went Quiet) *"Hey [Name], I saw your [event / news / update] and it reminded me of our earlier conversation. Still planning something similar?"*

Each opener accomplishes three things: relevance, curiosity, and invitation. No pressure, no pitch.

Adapting the Sales Linkage Process to Different Contexts

Enterprise or Multi-Decision Sales: When multiple stakeholders are involved, treat each contact as a unique customer with their own needs and priorities. Map the linkage chain separately for each person, the economic buyer, the end user, and the influencer often want different things from the same solution. Use shared summaries to align them as a group.

Transactional or Retail Sales: Condense the process. Connection and understanding happen quickly, sometimes in under two minutes. Focus on emotion and immediacy. Smile, serve, and simplify. The follow-through here might simply be a warm thank-you that keeps you remembered.

Digital or Remote Sales: Lead with clarity, remove extra words. Use visuals or short videos to humanize the interaction. Confirm understanding in writing to prevent confusion. And in every case, always leave with a clear next step.

Whatever the context, the rhythm stays the same:

Connect → Understand → Serve → Confirm → Continue.

Measurement and Momentum: Knowing What Matters

The goal of the Sales Linkage Process is not just more sales. It is better, longer, more trusted relationships. That means your metrics should measure *connection*, not just conversion.

Track the Behaviors That Predict Success

- Number of meaningful conversations (not just total dials)
- Positive outcomes: quotes, samples, orders (this is your pipeline)
- Number of follow-throughs completed on time
- Repeat customers or referrals this month
- Customer compliments, testimonials, or unsolicited praise

- Average response time to inquiries

Personal Weekly Review

Once a week, ask yourself these four questions honestly: 1. Did I listen more than I talked? 2. Did I add genuine value in every conversation? 3. Did I follow through on every promise I made? 4. Did I leave every person better than I found them?

That is the real scoreboard.

Continuous Learning and Adaptation

Markets evolve. Customers evolve. Your process must evolve with them. Stay curious — not occasionally, but as a professional standard:

- Read at least one new book on communication, psychology, or sales leadership each quarter.
- Revisit recorded calls and evaluate yourself against the Sales Linkage Process. Your own voice is your most honest coach.
- Ask peers and mentors for honest, specific feedback. Vague feedback produces vague growth.
- When a tactic stops working, adjust early — do not defend it past its usefulness.

Not everything will go as planned. Things will fall short. That is not failure — that is the job. Never abandon an entire program over a few misses when the critical priorities are being hit. Stay focused. Stay on process. Adjust where needed and keep moving.

PRO TIP: *Block one hour per week on your calendar and label it "Relationship Time." No admin. No meetings. No email. Just outreach to existing customers, check-ins, value shares, referral asks, thank-you notes. Protect it like it is your most important appointment, because it is. The salespeople who build extraordinary careers are not always the most talented in the room. They are usually the most consistent. That one hour per week compounds into something most salespeople never achieve: a loyal network that generates income without cold calls.*

Let's Review

- Manage time intentionally. Protect relationship time and batch administrative work.
- Use the Daily Power of 3, three openers, three follow-throughs, three improvements every day.
- Build a referral loop grounded in service, gratitude, and genuine connection.
- Adapt conversation openers to context, warm outreach, cold outreach, and re-engagement each have a different approach.
- Adapt the Sales Linkage Process to enterprise, retail, and digital environments. The rhythm stays the same, the format adjusts.
- Measure connection, not just conversion. Track the behaviors that predict long-term success.
- Learning, evolving, and refining, curiosity is a professional obligation.
- **Remember:** Structure plus humanity is where long-term success lives. Neither alone is enough.

Chapter 18: Your Sales Legacy — Leaving a Lasting Impact

How You Will Be Remembered as a Solutionist

The Question Behind the Career

When I first asked, *"Why do I need an umbrella?"* I did not realize that question would define so many careers beyond my own. It started as a teaching tool about listening, but it became something else entirely, a reminder that sales is a service. Service, done right, leaves a legacy.

I have had students remember that lesson years later. I have had people try to get my attention across an airport, yelling "Linkage!" Funny as that moment was, what stays with me is not the recognition. It is the thought that something in that room made an impact deep enough to follow someone into their daily life. That is the goal. That is what we are building toward.

Sales is more than a career. It is a skill, a calling, and an opportunity — every single day — to leave people better than you found them.

What Is a Sales Legacy?

A sales legacy is not the total revenue you generated or the number of deals you closed. It is the lasting impression you leave on the people you served, the trust you built, the problems you solved, and the lives you made genuinely easier.

When people think of you, they will remember:

- Someone asked questions before offering answers.
- A professional who followed through on every commitment.

- Someone who treated them like a person, not a transaction.
- A trusted advisor worthy of being recommended to their friends and colleagues.

Your legacy is shaped not by the biggest sale you ever made, but by how consistently you showed up with honesty, care, and a process that put the customer first.

"Legacy is built in the quiet choices: honesty, consistency, and gratitude."

The Ripple Effect of Great Sales

Every positive interaction creates ripples. A customer you served exceptionally well:

- Refers their colleagues, family, and friends to you — often without being asked.
- Becomes an advocate who talks about you with language your own marketing could never replicate.
- Returns for years, bringing their growing needs with them.

The team members you coached, the peers you invested in, and the new representatives you patiently taught will carry what you gave them into every conversation they have for the rest of their careers. That is influence at scale.

"Every conversation adds a link to your chain of influence."

For the Sales Leaders Reading This

Sales is a craft. Like any craft, it is easy to get comfortable doing simple work while avoiding the harder, messier parts. Coaching is one of the hardest and most important parts of leadership. It is also one of the biggest misses I see across the industry.

Too many leaders confuse coaching with reprimanding. A rep misses a QA score, and the leader swoops in to "coach", which really means pointing out the failure. That is not coaching. That is punishment, delivered after the fact. Real-time coaching happens *before* the failure, in real-time. It is proactive, not reactive. It is what prevents the poor QA score in the first place. In my next book called af2coaching.com we will tackle coaching and change culture, for the better.

If you are serious about leadership, you must invest in coaching. The majority of your time as a leader should be spent developing your people, through observations, one-on-ones, role-plays, and regular feedback loops. Coaching is not optional. It is not something you do when you have time. It *is* the job.

If you are not yet a leader, coach yourself. Review your hardest calls. Analyze what your most effective peers do well. Pick up their best objection-handling lines. Apply them to your own approach. Self-coaching is the seed of leadership.

"The best teams are never the ones with the most talent. They are the ones with the best coaching."

Moments That Matter

Legacy is not built in grand gestures or peak performances. It is built in small, quiet moments that often go unnoticed in real time:

The thank-you note you did not have to write. The customer who called three years later because you remembered what their logo looked like. The team members found their confidence because you took time to listen. The mistake you owned completely and turned into one of their strongest memories of you.

These moments may feel insignificant as they happen. Together, they form the story of your career. They are the emotional fingerprints you leave behind, proof points of consistency, character, and care.

Legacy is not what you do once. It is what you do repeatedly when no one is watching.

Your Legacy Starts Today

Every decision, every conversation, and every solution contributes to the legacy you are building right now. Integrity in the small moments. Honesty when it is inconvenient. Kindness when it is hard. Those are the choices that echo the longest.

Sales, leadership, and customer service are not just professional disciplines, they are human ones. Whether you are engaging with customers, mentoring employees, coaching a new rep, or simply showing someone that they were heard, the most meaningful interactions are grounded in something simple: genuine care.

On a personal note: remember the Golden Rule. Treat others the way you would want to be treated. In the sales conversation, in the follow-up, in the moment when something goes wrong. The energy you bring to your interactions either lifts people or diminishes them. Choose to lift. Be the light!

"Be the leader you have always wanted others to be to you. That is how cultures change. That is how legacies are built."

This book is only the beginning. Sales is a process and so are leadership, coaching, and customer service. I look forward to sharing more in my forthcoming books on leadership and coaching, where I will go deeper into the art of developing people, building high-performance cultures, and creating the kind of teams that deliver exceptional experiences every single day.

Until then: stay focused. Stay on process. Stay curious. Stay consistent. Stay human.

The Final Reflection

Sales began for many of us as a job, but it becomes something much greater. A reflection of who we are when no one is watching. Over time, the principles that built your success in sales, listening, serving, following through, become the same principles that define how you lead, how you love, and how you live.

The Umbrella Game taught us that people do not need to be persuaded. They need to be understood. The Sales Linkage Process showed us how to link needs to solutions with clarity and care. Every chapter has been about applying that truth in deeper, more meaningful ways, until selling stopped being about transactions and started being about transformation.

Your legacy will never be measured by how many deals you closed, but by how many people you lifted. The quiet choices, integrity when no one is watching, kindness when it is inconvenient, humility when it is hardest, are the ones that echo longest.

Take what you have learned here. Make it your own. Keep opening doors, building relationships, and linking every conversation to something that truly matters. You are now aware.

Good luck, God bless, and I wish you wild success.

Connect with Patrick

Patrick M. Arcement is available for speaking engagements, corporate sales training, leadership development, workshops, and **1-on-1 coaching sessions**.

Whether you are a sales professional looking to sharpen your process, a leader building a high-performing team, or an organization seeking to transform your customer experience, Patrick brings the Sales Linkage Process to life in ways that are practical, measurable, and lasting.

Reach Patrick directly:

- Personal site: patrickmarcement.com
- Book site & coaching: umbrellasalesbook.com
- Hire: arcementstrategygroup.com

Book owner discount: Use code **MyLinkage50** at umbrellasalesbook.com to save $50 on the full online course. Valid as long as the course is available. - Corporate training programs: saleslinkageprograms.com - AI technology solutions: repliantarc.com - Strategy & consulting: arcementstrategygroup.com

"Serve first. Success follows."

Sources and References

The following sources are cited or referenced throughout *SALES LINKAGE: Why Do I Need an Umbrella?* They are organized by chapter for ease of reference.

Preface and Chapter 1

Maya Angelou — "People will forget what you said, people will forget what you did, but people will never forget how you made them feel." This widely attributed quote appears across numerous published collections of Angelou's writings and interviews.

Microsoft Attention Span Study (2015) — A widely cited internal report from Microsoft Canada suggested that the average human attention span declined from approximately 12 seconds in 2000 to 8 seconds by 2015. The methodology of this study has been subject to debate in academic circles, and it is referenced here to illustrate a broadly observed trend rather than as a definitive scientific finding. Source: Microsoft Canada, *Attention Spans*, Consumer Insights, Spring 2015.

Chapter 2

Miller's Law / Rule of 7 — George A. Miller's landmark 1956 paper "The Magical Number Seven, Plus or Minus Two" established foundational research on human working memory capacity. Source: Miller, G.A. (1956). "The Magical Number Seven, Plus or Minus Two: Some Limits on Our Capacity for Processing Information." *Psychological Review*, 63(2), 81–97.

Chapter 3

PwC Customer Experience Study — Referenced finding that 73% of consumers consider the initial customer experience a critical factor in shaping their overall perception of a brand. Source: PwC, *Experience is Everything: Here's How to Get It Right*, 2018. Available at pwc.com.

Deloitte Customer Experience Research — Referenced finding that nearly 80% of customers evaluate every single interaction with a brand as an indicator of its overall quality. Source: Deloitte Insights, *The Value of Experience: How the C-Suite Values Customer Experience in the Digital Age*, 2017.

American Express Customer Service Barometer — Referenced finding that a dissatisfied customer is likely to share their negative experience with 15 or more people. Source: American Express, *2017 Customer Service Barometer*, conducted by Ebiquity.

Emergency Medical Technician Oath — The oath referenced in the paramedic story is a widely used version of the EMT pledge, derived from the National Registry of Emergency Medical Technicians and various state EMS training curricula.

Chapter 4

Customer Trust and Repeat Purchase Research — Referenced findings that 90% of consumers trust highly-rated companies and that 88% of customers are more likely to make repeat purchases from companies with excellent customer service. Source: Salesforce Research,

State of the Connected Customer, multiple editions (2018–2022). Available at salesforce.com.

Chapter 7

Cold Call Answer Rates — Industry research indicating cold call answer rates as low as 2–5%. Source: InsideSales.com (now XANT), *The Science of Sales*, and various industry benchmark reports from Rain Group and Gartner Sales Practice.

Door-to-Door Conversion Rates — Industry data indicating conversion rates between 1% and 3%. Source: Door-to-Door Sales industry benchmark reports; Spotio Sales Statistics, 2021.

Chapter 9

Mirror Listening and Anterior Insula — Referenced neuroscience research on how accurate reflection activates the anterior insula, the brain's empathy center. Source: Lamm, C., & Singer, T. (2010). "The role of anterior insular cortex in social emotions." *Brain Structure and Function*, 214(5–6), 579–591.

"Understood" and Brain Reward Centers — Referenced research that feeling understood activates the same reward centers as praise or gifts. Source: Zaki, J. (2014). "Empathy: A motivated account." *Psychological Bulletin*, 140(6), 1608–1647.

Chapter 10

The Zeigarnik Effect — Bluma Zeigarnik's foundational research on uncompleted tasks and mental tension. Source: Zeigarnik, B. (1927). "Über das Behalten von erledigten und unerledigten Handlungen." *Psychologische Forschung*, 9, 1–85.

Loss Aversion — Kahneman and Tversky — Referenced finding that losses feel roughly twice as painful as equivalent gains. Source: Kahneman, D., & Tversky, A. (1979). "Prospect Theory: An Analysis of Decision under Risk." *Econometrica*, 47(2), 263–292.

Chapter 11

First Responder Statistic — 78% Buy from First Responder — Referenced finding that 78% of customers buy from the company that responds first. Source: Velocify (now Velocify by Ellie Mae), *Lead Response Management Study*, 2012; also cited in LeadSimple and HubSpot research compilations.

Chapter 13 — The Power of Follow-Up

Brevet Group Follow-Up Statistics — Referenced findings that 80% of sales require at least five follow-ups and that 44% of salespeople give up after one follow-up. Source: Brevet Group, *Sales Follow Up Statistics*, cited widely in sales training literature. Original data sourced from Brevet Group sales effectiveness research, 2013–2018.

Chapter 14 — Navigating Objections

Loss Aversion — Kahneman and Tversky — See Chapter 10 reference above.

Chapter 15 — Building Lifelong Relationships

Redpoint Global Customer Loyalty Study — Referenced finding that 74% of consumers stay with a company because they feel understood and valued. Source: Redpoint Global, *The State of CX Maturity Among Midsize and Enterprise Businesses*, 2019.

Boomerang Email Study — Referenced analysis of 350,000 emails finding that emails ending with expressions of gratitude generated a 65.7% response rate compared to 46% for emails without a warm closing. Source: Boomerang, *How to End an Email: The Best and Worst Email Sign-Offs*, 2017. Available at boomeranggmail.com.

General References and Further Reading

The following works informed the broader psychological and behavioral framework of the Sales Linkage Process:

- Cialdini, R.B. (1984). *Influence: The Psychology of Persuasion.* Harper Business.
- Pink, D.H. (2012). *To Sell Is Human: The Surprising Truth About Moving Others.* Riverhead Books.
- Kahneman, D. (2011). *Thinking, Fast and Slow.* Farrar, Straus and Giroux.

- Carnegie, D. (1936). *How to Win Friends and Influence People.* Simon & Schuster.
- Blount, J. (2015). *Fanatical Prospecting.* Wiley.

Patrick M. Arcement has made every effort to accurately represent referenced research and attributed quotations. Readers who identify any inaccuracies are encouraged to contact the author at www.patrickmarcement.com

---

Legal Disclaimer

MyLinkage50 Discount Code — Terms of Use

The discount code MyLinkage50 is valid for $50 off the Sales Linkage online course at umbrellasalesbook.com. This code is intended for purchasers of the printed or digital edition of *SALES LINKAGE: Why Do I Need an Umbrella?* by Patrick M. Arcement. The code may be used one time per customer and has no cash value. The offer is valid only for the online course hosted at umbrellasalesbook.com and cannot be applied to coaching sessions, corporate training programs, live workshops, or any other products or services. Patrick M. Arcement and SparkUS Publications reserve the right to modify, suspend, or discontinue this offer at any time without notice.

Online Course — Important Notice

The Sales Linkage online course is delivered exclusively through the internet at umbrellasalesbook.com. A stable internet connection and a compatible web browser are required to access course materials. Course content, including modules and worksheets, is for personal use only and may not be reproduced, redistributed, resold, or shared without express written permission from Patrick M. Arcement.

General Disclaimer

The strategies, methods, and examples presented in this book and in the Sales Linkage online course are provided for educational and informational purposes only. Individual results will vary. Success in sales depends on many factors including but not limited to industry, market conditions, individual effort, experience, and the application of the principles taught. Neither Patrick M. Arcement nor SparkUS Publications makes any guarantee of specific results. Nothing in this book or course constitutes professional legal, financial, or business advice.

Glossary of Key Terms

The following terms are used throughout this book. They are defined here as Patrick uses them within the Sales Linkage framework.

Sales Linkage Process The five-step, psychology-backed sales framework created by Patrick M. Arcement. It connects customer needs to tailored solutions through structured questioning, active listening, and confident closing. The five steps are: Opening with Commitment, Identifying Needs, Prescribing Solutions, Securing Agreement, and Moving to Action.

My Commitment The opening statement a sales professional makes to establish their role, set expectations, and create a clear path forward in any sales conversation. Originally called "The Commitment," it becomes "My Commitment" when the salesperson internalizes and owns it as a personal promise rather than a procedural script.

Statement-Question Linked An active listening technique in which the salesperson restates what the customer just said and immediately links it to the next open-ended question. It validates the customer while advancing the conversation. Example: "So speed of delivery is critical for you. How much time would you ideally like to save?"

Needs-Based Selling A sales approach that prioritizes discovering what the customer actually needs before presenting any solution. The opposite of feature-dumping. The foundation of the Sales Linkage Process.

Feature-Dumping The common sales mistake of presenting product features or benefits before understanding what the customer needs. It overwhelms the customer and disconnects the solution from the problem.

The Weighted Scale A cost justification framework in which the salesperson helps the customer weigh the value of a solution against its cost. When value is clearly connected to the customer's stated needs, price becomes secondary.

Checking Questions Short, strategic questions used after presenting a solution to confirm the customer's agreement and reveal any remaining concerns. Examples: "Does this address what we discussed?" or "How does that sound to you?"

Action Statements Confident, forward-moving statements used to guide the customer into the next step once all needs have been addressed and agreement has been secured. Example: "Since this checks all your boxes, let's go ahead and finalize it for you."

The Umbrella Game A training exercise created by Patrick M. Arcement in which participants are given an umbrella store to run and challenged to discover why a customer truly needs an umbrella. The game teaches needs discovery by exposing how naturally salespeople default to marketing-style feature answers instead of asking questions.

Solutionist Patrick's term for a sales professional who prioritizes solving real problems over making transactions. A solutionist listens first, understands the need fully, and presents solutions with the customer's best interest at the center of every conversation.

The Customer Sentiment Health Bar A metaphor used in Chapter 3 to describe how every customer interaction either adds to or subtracts from the customer's overall trust and engagement. Borrowed from video game mechanics to illustrate that no interaction is neutral.

Cognitive Dissonance (in sales context) The mental discomfort a customer experiences between wanting something and fearing the decision to purchase it. Understanding this helps sales professionals respond with empathy rather than pressure.

Loss Aversion The psychological tendency for people to feel potential losses more strongly than equivalent gains. Referenced in the context of urgency and objection handling. First documented by psychologists Daniel Kahneman and Amos Tversky.

The Zeigarnik Effect The psychological phenomenon in which unfinished tasks create mental tension until resolved. In sales, this means customers are relieved when they finalize a decision, making completion itself a source of motivation.

Daily Power of 3 A daily productivity habit described in Chapter 17: three conversations to open, three follow-throughs to complete, and three improvements to make. Nine focused actions compounded daily produce sustained momentum.

Appendix — Scripts, Tools, and Reference Materials

The following materials are drawn directly from the chapters of this book. Use them as quick references, coaching tools, or training handouts.

Appendix A: My Commitment Script Template

Use this template to build your personal Commitment script. Practice it out loud until it sounds completely natural in your own voice.

Step 1 — Restate the known need: *"It would be my pleasure to help you find a solution that [restate what they came for in their own words]."*

Step 2 — Introduce yourself and your role: *"My name is [name], and I am a [your title or role]."*

Step 3 — Set expectations: *"Today I will ask you a few questions to better understand your situation…"*

Step 4 — Clarify the process: *"…so we can identify the best options tailored specifically to your needs."*

Step 5 — Define the path forward: *"Once you feel the solution meets your needs, we can move forward together. How does that sound?"*

Appendix B: Open-Ended Needs Discovery Questions

Use these questions during the Identifying Needs phase. Choose two or three per conversation. Never ask them all at once.

- What is most important to you when choosing [product or service]?
- Can you tell me about the challenges you are facing right now?
- What has worked well for you in the past, and what has not?
- How do you see this solution fitting into your goals?
- What is your biggest priority at the moment?
- What is your biggest challenge right now?
- Can you describe the ideal outcome for you?
- What has motivated you to explore this now?
- How does your current situation compare to what you would like it to be?

Appendix C: Common Objections and Responses

"That's too expensive." Restate the need, link the solution to the outcome, and show the math on value over time. Never apologize for your price.

"I need to think about it." Find the specific uncertainty: "Of course. Can I ask which part you are still considering? I would rather address that now."

"I can get it cheaper somewhere else." Acknowledge it and compare the real cost: "You absolutely can. Let me make sure you are comparing the same thing. The option you are referencing does not include [specific feature they said was important]."

"It is not in the budget right now." Keep the door open: "I understand. When would be a better time? And in the meantime, would a scaled option that delivers the core of what you need be helpful?"

"I need to talk to my spouse or boss." Prepare them: "That makes total sense. What do you think their biggest concern might be? If we address that now, you will walk into that conversation with all the answers."

Appendix D: Action Statements

Use these after all needs have been addressed and the customer has confirmed agreement.

- "Since this checks all your boxes, let's go ahead and finalize it for you."
- "Everything lines up with what you need. Let's lock this in."
- "You mentioned wanting this in place by [date]. Let's get started so we hit that timeline."
- "Great choice. Let's make it official."
- "This solution fits everything we talked about. Let's move forward."

Appendix E: Follow-Up Message Templates

Within 24 to 48 hours after the sale: "Thank you for trusting me to help you with [specific solution]. I am genuinely excited about the positive impact this will have for you. Please reach out any time."

Shortly after delivery: "I wanted to check in and see how things are going with [product or service]. Is there anything I can help with?"

Periodic relationship check-in: "It has been a while since we last connected. I wanted to check in and see how things are going. Are there any new challenges I can help you solve?"

Re-engagement for quiet contacts: "I thought of you when [relevant update or news]. Still planning something similar to what we discussed?"

Appendix F: The Sales Linkage Process — Quick Reference

Step	Name	Core Action
1	Opening with Commitment	Introduce yourself, establish expertise, state My Commitment
2	Identifying Needs	Ask open-ended questions, uncover 3 to 5 real needs
3	Prescribing Solutions	Link one solution to one need at a time
4	Securing Agreement	Use checking questions, gather yes responses

Step	Name	Core Action
5	Moving to Action	Use confident action statements to guide forward

Remember: Marketing tells. Sales asks. If you are telling, you are not selling.

Visit **umbrellasalesbook.com** for more details.

www.ingramcontent.com/pod-product-compliance
Lightning Source LLC
LaVergne TN
LVHW010623100826
845148LV00014B/3076

* 9 7 9 8 2 3 4 0 5 3 2 6 8 *